30 Minute
Air Fryer Cookbook
with
Full Color Pictures

**Time Saving Recipes For Beginners
To Cook Easy & Simple Delicious
Homemade Meals Everyday**

Culinary Press

TABLE OF CONTENTS

Introduction   6

    What Is an Air Fryer?   7

    How Does an Air Fryer Work?   7

    Benefits of Using an Air Fryer   7

    Other Benefits   8

    Air Fryer Buying Guide   8

    Air Fryer Q&A   10

    Air Fryer Cooking Techniques   11

    Air Fryer Conversion   11

    General Air Fryer Cooking Chart   12

Chapter 1 – Breakfast Recipes   13

    Maple Glazed Bliss Apple Fritters   14

    Choco Berry Pancakes   15

    Protein-Packed Breakfast Burritos   16

    Warm Spiced Vanilla French Toast Sticks   17

    Veggie Overload Breakfast Frittata   18

    Flaky Sausage Egg Pouches   19

    Eggscellent Scotch Bites   20

    Sunny Stuffed Breakfast Spuds   21

    Morning Egg Roll Fiesta   22

    Blueberry Euphoria Scones   23

Chapter 2 – Poultry Recipes   24

    Golden Roasted Chicken Thighs   25

    Thai Tango Chicken Satay   26

    Divine Chicken Parmesan   27

    Smoky Garlic Chicken Wings   28

    7-Spice Fried Chicken   29

    Honey Garlic Chicken Drumsticks   30

    Sizzling Sunset Chicken Fajitas   31

    Enchanted Chicken Enchiladas   32

    Tokyo Nights Chicken Yakitori   33

    Zesty Lemon Pepper Turkey Wings   34

    Gobble Gobble Turkey Meatballs   35

    Mediterranean Style Turkey Burgers   36

    Cajun Turkey Tenderloin with Maple Glaze   37

Chapter 3 – Beef & Pork Recipes 38

Sweet and Spicy Mongolian Beef 39
Gourmet Perfection Filet Mignon 40
Succulent Beef and Broccoli Medley 41
BBQ Cheddar Burgers 42
Sweet Chili BBQ Meatloaf 43
Carnivore's Delight Beef Kabobs 44
Opa! Zeus Meatballs 45
Savory Pork Chop Perfection 46
Sizzling Harmony BBQ Ribs 47
Cheesy Sausage Ziti 48
Honey Mustard Pork Tenderloin 49
Sausage-Infused Mushroom Delight 50

Chapter 4 – Seafood Recipes 51

Dill and Basil Salmon 52
Spicy Cajun Shrimp and Vegetables 53
Crispy Golden Fish Sticks 54
Easy Air Fryer Bacon-Wrapped Scallops 55
Sweet Smoky Salmon Bites 56
Crispy Fish Sandwich 57
Seafood Bliss Shrimp Tacos 58
The Ultimate Crab Cakes 59
Flaky Tilapia with Garlic and Lemon Pepper 60
Lemon Garlic Butter Lobster Tails 61
Sweet Umami Honey-Glazed Salmon 62
Crunchy Tender Calamari 63

Chapter 5 – Vegetable Mains and Sides Recipes 64

Crispy Broccoli 65
Soy Garlic Brussels Sprouts 66
Parmesan and Herb Sweet Potatoes 67
Spicy Cauliflower 68
Delightfully Crispy French Fries 69
Chili Sweet Potato Fries 70
Zesty Green Beans 71
Sweet and Buttery Corn on the Cob 72
Savory Herbed Carrots 73
Crispy Avocado Tacos 74
Herb-Roasted Vegetable Medley 75
Four Ingredient Veggie Pasta Bake 76

Chapter 6 – Bread and Snack Recipes   77

Parmesan Garlic Bread 78
Smoky BBQ Potato Chips 79
Ranch Kale Chips 80
Cajun Portobello Mushroom Fries 81
Buffalo Cauliflower 82
Parmesan Avocado Fries 83
Cheesy Crispy Ravioli with Warm Marinara Sauce 84
Simple Cheddar Herb Bread 85
Blueberry Lemon Bread 86
Classic Pizza Bagels 87
Classic Mozzarella Sticks 88

Chapter 7 – Dessert Recipes   89

Air Fryer Chocolate Chip Cookies 90
Crunchy Cinnamon Churros 91
Decadently Rich Brownies 92
Molten Magic Lava Cake 93
Cranberry Walnut Bread Pudding 94
Warm Cinnamon Rolls 95
Sweet Nebula Fried Oreos 96
Nutty Nirvana Peanut Butter Cookies 97
Lazy No-Rise Doughnuts 98
Spiced Peach Cobbler 99
Apple Pie Bombs 100

Conclusion **101**
Recipe Index **102**
Ingredients Index **104**
References **105**

YOUR FREE BONUS GIFTS

Thank you for purchasing our cookbook!
We are thrilled to offer you the following gifts:

EXTRA 50+ 30 MINUTE AIR FRYER BONUS RECIPES

THE ULTIMATE AIR FRYER GUIDE

Grab these Extra 50 bonus air fryer recipes! Each recipe contains:

- Takes 30-minutes to make recipes
- Uses easy-to-find ingredients
- Has clear instructions
- Has images to show you what the recipe should look like
- Has cooking time, serving sizes, and nutritional information
- Contains little to no oil

Grab this bonus guide! You will learn how to:

- Use your air fryer safely
- Air fryer tips and tricks
- How to clean your air fryer
- The best air fryer accessories
- The best and worst oils and pump spray

You can visit https://culinarypressbooks.com/free-gift1 to get these gifts or scan the QR code. In addition to your gifts, you'll also have access to exclusive giveaways, discounts, and other valuable information.

Email us if you have any issues accessing the bonuses at contact@culinarypressbooks.com
Thanks again for purchasing our cookbook.

Sincerely,

The Culinary Press Team

INTRODUCTION

Forget what you've been told about air fryers because it's probably all a lie! You've probably spent money on cookbooks that claim to be the best but are filled with useless recipes that can't even be cooked in the air fryer. You may not even be able to use the recipes because they are not tailored to your air fryer's size.

Maybe you came across cookbooks with recipes containing foods like zucchini fries and fried pickles that no one wants to eat. We could go on and on about the unclear instructions, fancy meals that take forever to cook, or foods drenched in oil when you don't really need it. We understand your pain. We are also tired of wasting time and money on poorly written cookbooks that serve no purpose.

Sure, you could buy the average black-and-white air fryer cookbook with more than 600 recipes (that the author never even made), but let's be real. You are not going to eat more than 600 recipes. You want a few delicious go-to recipes that are easy to make in 30 minutes or less.

So, if you truly want the best air fryer experience, this is the only cookbook you need. The team at Culinary Press, as well as our family and friends, have tested more than 500 air fryer recipes and narrowed them down to the top 81.

We value quantity over quality. That's why you won't find a better cookbook than this air fryer cookbook with full-color pictures of every meal. The dishes are so easy to make; even a person who has never cooked a dish before can prepare a delicious meal in 30 minutes or less. Each recipe contains the exact air fryer size needed to make the meal, a list of all the ingredients, precise nutritional values, and customary and metric measurements.

We're about to turn everything you thought you knew about air frying on its head. No more feeling like you got bamboozled or wasted your money. This cookbook is not the average air fryer cookbook. It's not filled with complicated recipes using ingredients you have never heard of. It is crafted by a team of culinary experts.

At Culinary Press, we aim to craft the best cookbooks in the world. Our chefs, culinary experts, and writers are dedicated to bringing the joy of cooking into homes, fostering creativity, and elevating your kitchen experience, even if you are a newbie to cooking. This air fryer cookbook is no different. Our skilled authors bring a wealth of knowledge and experience, ensuring that this air fryer cookbook is a valuable resource.

This cookbook is tailored to make your air frying experience a breeze. It does not contain complicated recipes, hard-to-find ingredients, or unclear instructions. Just straightforward, easy-to-follow recipes that will turn you into an air frying pro in no time. Whether you're a beginner or a seasoned chef, our cookbook is designed to simplify the art of air frying, giving you the confidence to create mouthwatering dishes that are delicious and nutritious.

Brace yourself because your air fryer is about to become your kitchen sidekick, and we're here to guide you every step of the way. So, buckle up and get ready to savor the delights of air frying like never before! Let's go!

WHAT IS AN AIR FRYER?

An air fryer is a kitchen appliance used to cook foods with little to no oil. Air fryers typically have a heating element and a fan that rapidly circulates hot air within the cooking chamber.

Although the word "fry" is in the name, air fryers are not traditional fryers. They are more like small convection ovens on steroids. The difference is convection ovens are large and take forever to heat up. They require installation by professionals. Air fryers are small countertop cookers. They heat up in a few minutes and cook foods faster than convection ovens.

HOW DOES AN AIR FRYER WORK?

Air fryers use radiant heat and convection to prepare your food. Most air fryers contain a heating element at the top of the appliance. However, the heating element can be at the bottom of the cooker in larger air fryers.

Food is arranged in a basket or rack that goes into the air fryer. The heating element heats the cooking chamber (radiation). The fan circulates the hot air rapidly around the food (convection), cooking the food from all angles and giving it a crisp texture.

BENEFITS OF USING AN AIR FRYER

Air fryers don't just simply make your life easier. They also help you lead healthier lifestyles.

- **Reduced oil consumption**

One of the main benefits of an air fryer is that it allows you to cook with significantly less oil compared to traditional frying methods. Traditional fried foods are deep-fried in unhealthy fats. Eating large amounts of fried foods may increase your risk of developing cardiovascular disease (Qin et al., 2021). Consuming less oil can contribute to a lower intake of unhealthy fats, which is associated with a reduced risk of cardiovascular diseases.

- **Lower calorie intake**

Since air-fried foods have a reduced fat content, they are generally lower in calories. This can be beneficial for individuals looking to lose weight, manage their weight, or reduce calorie intake without sacrificing flavor and texture.

- **Decreased formation of harmful compounds**

Traditional deep-frying can lead to the formation of potentially harmful compounds, such as acrylamide. Oil heated to extremely high temperatures may lead to the breakdown of products, especially when cooking starchy foods such as fries at high temperatures. Acrylamide is regarded as a potential carcinogen and ranked

Group 2A (likely carcinogenic to humans) by the International Agency for Research on Cancer (Kuek et al., 2020). Air frying at lower temperatures may help minimize the formation of these compounds, promoting a healthier cooking process and potentially reducing exposure to harmful compounds.

- **Nutrient retention**

Cooking methods such as boiling, which involves prolonged exposure to heat, can decrease the amount of nutrients that are absorbed and used by the body (Coe & Spiro, 2022). Also, many water-soluble nutrients are lost when the cooking water is discarded. Air fryers have shorter cooking times and lower temperatures. Therefore, air frying may help retain more nutrients in food than other cooking methods.

OTHER BENEFITS

The benefits of the air fryer go beyond health. Air fryers make cooking easier.

- **Versatility**

Air fryers are versatile appliances that can handle a wide range of foods, including fish, fries, chicken, vegetables, and even desserts. Some models also come with additional features like grilling, roasting, dehydrating, and baking functions, expanding your cooking options. This versatility encourages the preparation of a variety of nutritious meals with different cooking techniques.

- **Saves time**

Air fryers cook food faster than traditional methods, reducing overall cooking time. The rapid hot air circulation speeds up the cooking process. Air frying is a convenient option for busy individuals or those who want to prepare quick, healthy meals in 30 minutes or less.

- **Easy to use**

Air fryers are generally easy to use. Most are designed with simple controls and minimal preheating time. They also have presets for common dishes, making it convenient for users to achieve consistent results without needing extensive culinary skills.

- **Less mess**

Air fryers use less oil than traditional frying methods and have a contained cooking chamber. You don't have to worry about getting splattered by hot oil or accidentally spilling or severe burns from hot oil. There is less mess compared to traditional frying.

- **Energy efficient**

Most air fryers are more energy-efficient than traditional ovens. Their compact size and shorter cooking times cook foods faster, contributing to reduced energy consumption.

AIR FRYER BUYING GUIDE

Everyone wants to know what type of air fryer they should buy. It depends on your specific needs, as well as your budget and space capacity. For example, you may want an air fryer with presets. You may want an air fryer that costs less than $100 or a larger air fryer that can cook for a family of six. Let's take a look at the types of air fryers to help you figure out which one is right for you.

Types of air fryers

There are two main types of air fryers: basket-style and oven or rack-style. Basket-style air fryers have a detachable basket you can pull out. Rack-style air fryers are mini ovens that cook food faster. They are designed with 2-3 oven-style racks you can use together or separately.

Let's explore the pros and cons of each type.

BASKET-STYLE AIR FRYERS

PROS
- Smaller, so it takes up less space
- Heats up and cooks food fast
- Handy if you have a small kitchen or live in an apartment
- You can shake the basket instead of turning your food over.
- Easier to clean than some of the wire racks in the oven-style air fryer

CONS
- Can only prepare small servings of food. Some larger 5-6 qt. models can cook four (6 oz.) salmon fillets or steaks.
- Food burns more easily if it is too close to the upper heating element.
- Can only cook one type of food item at a time.

OVEN STYLE AIR FRYERS

PROS
- You can cook larger portions and cuts of meat like roast beef or prime rib.
- Some oven-style air fryers come with 2-3 racks that allow you to rotate food so it can cook evenly.
- You can prepare different types of food, such as steak and fries, at the same time, with 2-3 racks if they have the same cooking temperature. You can place foods with the shortest cooking time on the top and those that take longer to cook on the bottom rack.
- Most oven-style air fryers are multi-cookers. You can air fry, broil, cook meat on a rotisserie, bake, dehydrate, and roast foods. You can even proof bread in these air fryers.

CONS
- It's larger. It takes more time to heat up and cook food.
- You have to turn the food over instead of shaking the basket.
- You have to preheat it before placing the food in the air fryer.
- Designed with wire racks, which are harder to clean.
- Takes up a lot of counter space.
- This model costs more money. However, this can be a benefit if you plan to use it a lot.

AIR FRYER SIZES

Now that we have discussed the types of air fryers, let's talk about sizes. Air fryers come in several sizes. Some are large while others are smaller. Let's discuss each size in depth so you can decide which size is best for you.

- ### 4 L Air Fryer
A 4 L air fryer is perfect for 2-3 people. They range from small to medium. However, they are large enough to prepare 2-3 portions of food, depending on what you are cooking. For example, you can cook two to three pieces of boneless pork chops in one batch. Also, 4 L air fryers won't take up too much space on your countertop, so they are ideal for small kitchens.

- ### 12 L Air Fryer
This size is perfect for cooking larger vegetables like carrots, zucchini, and eggplants. While this air fryer is quite large, it's not big enough to cook a whole chicken, so you may need a bigger model if you want to cook large cuts of meat.

- ### 16 L Air Fryer
A 16 L fryer is an extra-large. They are perfect for cooking for 4 or more people. These powerful machines have different cooking settings, like roasting and dehydrating. They are also ideal for making baked goods like cakes and roasting large items like whole chicken.

- ### Extra-Large 25 L Air Fryer Oven
Bigger air fryers allow you to use more cooking methods to prepare food. You can prepare nearly anything in this air fryer. Thanks to its large size, you can make baked goods, fries, steak, and even apple chips. Bigger air fryers cost more and take up a lot of space, so keep this in mind if you are considering buying one.

Ultimately, the perfect air fryer will depend on your specific needs. Ask yourself these five questions before making your purchase:

1. How much money am I willing to spend?
2. How many people will I be cooking for?
3. How much space do I have?
4. What features must my air fryer have (e.g., presets, a knob and dial, or a touch screen)?
5. What type of food do I want to cook in it?

Based on your responses, choose the air fryer that is best for you.

AIR FRYER & Q&A

It's only natural that you have questions about your air fryer. Here are the most frequently asked questions about these appliances.

What foods can't be air fried?

Not every food can be air-fried. Wet battered foods like tempura or beer battered are not suitable. Light foods such as spinach are not suitable because they fly around in the air fryer due to the convection fan. Popcorn should not be cooked in the air fryer either. Most air fryers don't generate enough heat to pop the corn. If they do, there is a risk of the popcorn touching the heating element, which can produce white smoke.

Can I air-fry frozen chicken?

Yes, you can air fry frozen chicken in the air fryer. You can cook frozen chicken breasts, thighs, wings, and legs. The food will take a little longer to cook, but it will be perfectly delicious.

Can I use butter in an air fryer?

Technically, you can use butter in an air fryer. However, butter has a low smoke point, so it's best to use just small amounts since it can make your air fryer smoke if it touches the heating element. Alternatively, you can add a small amount of water to the bottom of the basket to prevent the air fryer from smoking.

How do I prevent food from sticking to my air fryer basket?

Some foods, such as breaded chicken or fish, are prone to sticking to the air fryer basket or racks. Spray the air fryer basket lightly with oil to prevent this. Alternatively, you can also use perforated parchment paper or create boats from foil.

How much food can an air fryer hold?

The exact capacity of your air fryer depends on its size. The average air fryer can prepare about two to four servings of food. Remember not to overcrowd the basket. You can always cook food in batches instead.

Do I need to purchase accessories?

Accessories expand your air fryer's capabilities. For example, some air fryer manufacturers offer racks, skewers, and baking pans. This allows you to make cakes, kabobs, pancakes, and more. You can also cook different foods at the same time with the racks. So, the accessories are definitely worth the extra investment.

Can I use foil?

You can use foil in the air fryer. However, some air fryer models are not designed to be used with foil. Check your manual to see if you can use foil in your model. Additionally, you have to follow these rules when using foil in the air fryer. First, it must not block the flow of air if you want the food to develop a crispy texture. For example, wrapping your food with foil will prevent it from crisping up. Second, do not preheat the air fryer with foil in it. The foil must be weighted down with food, or it will blow around and touch the heating instrument, which may cause a fire and destroy your air fryer. Third, do not use foil if you are cooking acidic foods. This may cause chemicals in the foil to leach into your food.

Can I use wax paper?

You should never put wax paper in your air fryer or any oven. Wax paper isn't heat-safe. Since the air fryer rapidly circulates hot air, the wax on the paper will melt.

Can I use metal utensils?

Yes, unlike with a microwave, you can use metal in your air fryer. However, metal utensils may damage the basket's non-stick coating. For this reason, it's best to use wooden or silicone utensils.

How often should I clean my air fryer?

Clean your air fryer every time you use it. You don't have to deep clean it after each use, but it is best to rinse off the racks or trays and wipe down the basket with a damp cloth. However, if you have prepared something messy, you'll need to remove the racks and trays from the appliance and clean them with hot, soapy water.

AIRFRYER COOKING TECHNIQUES

Air fryers are versatile appliances that can be used for various cooking techniques beyond just frying. Here are some popular cooking techniques you can explore:

1. Air frying

This technique is used to mimic the effects of deep-frying food in oil by using little to no oil. Hot air circulates rapidly around the food, cooking it on all sides and creating a crispy exterior. This method is perfect for cooking foods like French fries, chicken wings, and vegetable chips. It's also great for reheating food. It can bring back the crispiness of leftover items like pizza, fried chicken, or even spring rolls.

2. Roasting & baking

The roast setting is a higher-temperature way of roasting meats and vegetables. Baking uses a lower temperature to ensure foods such as cakes, cookies, cupcakes, whole chicken, or turkey are cooked you are wondering what the difference between roasting and baking is, they are the same in a sense. For example, you set the oven to a specific temperature and cook the food for a set time when roasting and baking. However, the term "baking" refers to baked goods like cakes, cookies, muffins, and bread. "Roasting" refers to meats, potatoes, and other vegetables.

3. Grilling

Grilling applies direct radiant heat to the food. Some air fryers come with grill pans or accessories that allow you to achieve grill marks on meats and vegetables. This technique imparts a smoky flavor without using an outdoor grill.

4. Broiling

Like grilling, broiling uses radiant heat to cook food quickly. However, the heating element is located above the food. If your air fryer has a top heating element, you can broil food. This function is great for browning casseroles and cooking bacon on high heat for short periods.

5. Dehydrating

Turn your air fryer into a dehydrator by using low temperatures to remove moisture from fruits, vegetables, or even herbs. Make your own dried snacks without the need for additional equipment.

6. Toasting

Reheat or toast bread, bagels, or even leftover pizza in the air fryer. It's a quick way to achieve a crispy texture without using a traditional toaster.

7. Rotisserie

Some air fryers come with rotisserie attachments, allowing you to cook a whole chicken, prime rib, or other meats on a rotating spit. This technique ensures even cooking and crispy skin.

AIR FRYER CONVERSION

Converting regular recipes into air fryer recipes is easier than you think. Just follow these 4 simple rules.

1. Find the recipe you want to convert.
2. Look for the oven cooking temperature and the cooking time.
3. Decrease the oven cooking temperature by 25 degrees and the cooking time by 20 percent. This may seem like not enough time to cook the food, but remember the radiant heat and hot air circulation will cook the food faster than the oven.
4. Check your dish every so often and adjust the cooking time as necessary.

This same formula works with deep frying foods also. So, if you have a deep-fried chicken wing recipe that calls for deep frying wings at 350°F, you would air fry the chicken wings at 325°F.

GENERAL AIR FRYER COOKING CHART

*Note: Cooking times may vary from recipes because in this cookbook we are trying to save you as much time as possible. These are just general guidelines for cooking temps in an air fryer.

CHICKEN

Food	Temp.	Cooking Time
Chicken Tenders	400°F	14-16 minutes
Bone-in Chicken Thighs (1 lb.)	400°F	25 minutes
Boneless Chicken Thighs (1 lb.)	380°F	15-18 minutes
Chicken Wings (1 lb.)	375°F	10-12 minutes
Chicken Legs (1 lb.)	390°F	25 minutes
Leg Quarters (2 pieces)	380°F	20-25 minutes
Bone-in Chicken Breasts (1 lb.)	375°F	22-23 minutes
Boneless Chicken Breast (4 oz.)	380°F	12-16 minutes
Whole Chicken	350°F	70-75 minutes
Cornish Game Hen	350°F	35-37 minutes

BEEF

Food	Temp.	Cooking Time
Meatballs	400°F	7-10 minutes
Meat Loaf	325°F	35-45 minutes
Burgers (4 oz.)	350°F	8-10 minutes
Filet Mignon (6 oz.)	450°F	10 minutes
Brats	400°F	8-10 minutes
Flank Steak (1 lb.)	400°F	12-15 minutes
Ribeye Steak (8 oz.)	400°F	7-14 minutes
London Broil (1 ½ lbs.)	400°F	8-10 minutes

PORK

Food	Temp.	Cooking Time
Bone-In Pork Chops (1 lb.)	400°F	12 minutes
Boneless Pork Chops (1 lb.)	400°F	12 minutes
Pork Tenderloin	400°F	11-14 minutes
Pork loin (2 lb.)	360°F	12-15 minutes
Sausage Patties	400°F	8-10 minutes

SEAFOOD

Food	Temp.	Cooking Time
Cod (4 oz..)	370°F	8-10 minutes
Salmon (4 oz.)	400°F	5-7 minutes
Shrimp	375°F	8 minutes
Tilapia	400°F	6-8 minutes
Calamari	400°F	7 minutes

LAMB

Food	Temp.	Cooking Time
Lamb Loin Chops (1 ½ lbs.)	400°F	7-9 minutes
Lamb Leg Roast (10 oz.)	360°F	15-20 minutes
Rack Of Lamb (1 ½ lbs.)	350°F	22 minutes

FROZEN FOODS

Food	Temp.	Cooking Time
Mozzarella Sticks	400°F	6-8 minutes
Frozen Fries	400°F	10 minutes
Corn Dogs	400°F	8 minutes
Tater Tots	400°F	12-15 minutes

VEGETABLES

Food	Temp.	Cooking Time
Sweet Potatoes (cubed)	375°F	15-20 minutes
Asparagus	375°F	4-6 minutes
Baked Potatoes	400°F	35-45 minutes
Butternut Squash (cubed)	375°F	20-25 minutes
Green Beans	375°F	16-20 minutes
Broccoli	400°F	8-10 minutes
Zucchini	400°F	12 minutes
Cauliflower	400°F	10-12 minutes
Carrots	375°F	15-25 minutes
Peppers	375°F	8-10 minutes
Brussels Sprouts	350°F	15-18 minutes
Fries	400°F	10-20 minutes
Potato Chips	360°F	15-17 minutes

BAKED GOODS

Food	Temp.	Cooking Time
Brownies	325°F	40-45 minutes
Cake	320°F	30 minutes
Cupcakes	325°F	11-13 minutes
Cookies	325°F	8-10 minutes
Canned Biscuits	330°F	10 minutes
Scones	320°F	15 minutes
Muffins	325°F	11-12 minutes
Homemade Biscuits	325°F	10-12 minutes

We have discussed everything you need to know about air frying food. From tips and tricks to an air fryer buying guide and answering your burning questions about air fryers, we've covered it all. Now it's time to move on to the part you are probably most excited about: the recipes.

We have included 81 recipes that include every category you can think of. From breakfast to beef and pork and dessert recipes, there is something for everyone in this cookbook. So, let's get cooking!

CHAPTER 1
BREAKFAST RECIPES

MAPLE GLAZED BLISS APPLE FRITTERS

Prep Time
10 MINUTES

Cook Time
20 MINUTES

Total Time
30 MINUTES

Serves
10 FRITTERS

INGREDIENTS

Brown Butter Maple Glaze

- ¼ cup (1/2 stick or 57 grams) unsalted butter
- ½ cup (160 ml) maple syrup
- ⅔ cups (75 grams) powdered sugar
- 1 teaspoon (5 ml) vanilla extract

Apple Fritters

- 1 ½ cups (170 grams) whole wheat flour
- ¼ cup (50 grams) granulated sugar
- Zest of 1 lemon
- 2 teaspoons (10 grams) baking powder
- ¼ teaspoon (1.5 grams) fine sea salt
- 1 ½ teaspoons (3 grams) ground cinnamon
- ⅓ cup (77 ml) unsweetened apple cider
- 1 teaspoon (5 ml) vanilla extract
- 1 tablespoon (15 ml) fresh lemon juice
- 2 large eggs
- 2 large Granny Smith apples, peeled, cored, diced small
- Avocado oil for misting

NUTRITION INFO

SERVING SIZE: 1 APPLE FRITTER

Calories	124 kcal
Carbohydrates	26.8g
Fats	1.3g
Protein	2g
Sugar	20.1g
Sodium	55mg
Cholesterol	36mg

INSTRUCTIONS

Brown Butter Maple Glaze

1. Place the butter in a small pan, set it over medium-high heat, and let it melt.
2. Cook it for 2-3 minutes, stirring often until it begins to foam, turns brown, and has a nutty aroma. Pour the browned butter into a bowl.
3. Add the maple syrup, powdered sugar, and vanilla extract. Whisk until a smooth glaze forms. Set it aside.

Apple Fritters

1. Preheat the air fryer to 400°F (204°C).
2. Whisk the whole wheat flour, granulated sugar, lemon zest, baking powder, fine sea salt, and ground cinnamon in a large bowl until combined.
3. Make a well in the center of the dry ingredients, add the unsweetened apple cider, vanilla extract, lemon juice, and eggs, and stir with a wooden spoon until combined.
4. Fold in the Granny Smith apples until combined.
5. Line the basket with parchment paper (make sure it fits the bottom of the air fryer so it does not overlap) and mist it lightly with avocado oil.
6. Place 1/4 cup (60 grams) of apple fritter batter into the air fryer basket or tray. Repeat to add 5-6 more apple fritters to the air fryer.
7. Bake the apple fritters for 4-5 minutes at 400°F (204°C). Flip them over and cook them for another 4-5 minutes until golden brown.
8. Place the apple fritters on a cooling rack and repeat steps 6-7 until all the batter is gone.
9. Drizzle the apple fritters with the browned butter maple glaze before serving.

Notes

- This recipe is designed for a 16 L air fryer rack oven or extra-large 25L air fryer oven.
- You can cook the apple fritters in 3-4 batches (3-4 apple fritters at a time) in a 12L basket-style air fryer or 5-6 batches (2 apple fritters at a time) in a 4L air fryer basket-style air fryer.
- If you are cooking the apple fritters in a larger air fryer, be careful not to overcrowd the basket and increase the cooking time to 14-15 minutes, checking on the fritters every 4 minutes.
- Store the apple fritters in an airtight container at room temperature for 2 days.

Tips

1. Cut the butter into pieces. This will prevent it from spattering and burning and help it cook more evenly.
2. Use a heavy-bottomed light-colored pan to make the browned butter. This pan will distribute the heat better, helping it to cook more evenly. You will be able to see when the milk solids start to brown, so you can remove the browned butter from the stove at the right time.
3. Tart apples help balance out the sweet flavor of the fritter and browned butter maple glaze. However, you can use sweet varieties like honey crisp or Braeburn apples if desired.

CHOCO BERRY PANCAKES

Prep Time	Cook Time	Total Time	Serves
10 MINUTES	**7 MINUTES**	**17 MINUTES**	**4 PANCAKES**

INGREDIENTS

- 1 ¼ cups (150 grams) whole wheat flour
- 1 teaspoon (5 grams) baking powder
- 1 teaspoon (5 grams) orange zest
- ½ teaspoon (3 grams) baking soda
- ¼ teaspoon (1.5 grams) fine sea salt
- 2 tablespoons (30 ml) maple syrup
- 1 ⅓ cups (323 ml) buttermilk
- 1 large egg
- 1 tablespoon (15 ml) avocado oil
- ½ cup (80 grams) mini chocolate chips
- ½ cup (95 grams) fresh blueberries

NUTRITION INFO

SERVING SIZE: 1 PANCAKE

Calories	178 kcal
Carbohydrates	25.6 g
Fats	7.1 g
Protein	7.1 g
Sugar	14.2 g
Sodium	167 mg
Cholesterol	49 mg

INSTRUCTIONS

1. Mix the whole wheat flour, baking powder, orange zest, baking soda, and sea salt in a large bowl until combined.

2. Whisk the maple syrup, buttermilk, egg, and avocado oil in a separate bowl until combined. Pour it into the dry ingredients and mix until combined.

3. Fold in the chocolate chips and blueberries until combined.

4. Let the batter rest for 5 minutes while you preheat your air fryer to 370°F (187°C) for 3-5 minutes.

5. Mist a 6-inch (15 cm) aluminum cake pan with oil. Add 1/2 cup (80 grams) of pancake batter to the pan and spread it into an even circle.

6. Place the pancake in the air fryer basket and bake it for 6-7 minutes until golden brown.

7. Remove the pan from the air fryer and invert the pancake onto a cooling rack.

8. Repeat steps 5-7 to cook the remaining pancakes and serve with your desired toppings.

Notes

- This recipe is designed to cook 1 pancake at a time in a 4 L or 12 L air fryer basket-style air fryer.

- You can cook pancakes in 16 L or an extra-large 25 L rack-style air fryer. Depending on the height of the racks, you may be able to cook 2 pancakes at a time.

Tips

1. Do not use an aluminum pan that has a nonstick coating. It will cause the pancakes to have a domed surface instead of a flat one.

2. You can also cook the pancakes in silicone air fryer muffin pans. This will allow you to cook 3 pancakes at once. However, you will invert the pancakes directly onto the air fryer basket or rack after 5 minutes and cook them for another 4-5 minutes until golden brown.

3. If you aren't eating the pancakes right away, place them in a 200°F oven until you are ready to serve them.

PROTEIN-PACKED BREAKFAST BURRITOS

Prep Time
10 MINUTES

Cook Time
20 MINUTES

Total Time
30 MINUTES

Serves
4 BURRITOS

INGREDIENTS

- 1 tablespoon (15 ml) olive oil
- 1 medium russet potato, peeled, diced small
- 1 teaspoon (5 grams) kosher salt
- ½ teaspoon (1.5 grams) black pepper
- 3 tablespoons (45 ml) water
- ½ lb. (227 grams) raw lean turkey breakfast sausage
- 3 large eggs
- 3 tablespoons (45 ml) whole milk
- ¾ cup (85 grams) shredded cheddar cheese
- 4 flour tortillas
- Avocado oil for misting

NUTRITION INFO

SERVING SIZE: 1 BURRITO

Calories	407 kcal
Carbohydrates	44 g
Fats	16.7 g
Protein	21.6 g
Sugar	6.7 g
Sodium	809 mg
Cholesterol	153 mg

INSTRUCTIONS

1. Place the olive oil in a large skillet and set it over medium-high heat. Add the potatoes to the skillet and cook them for 2 minutes. Add the ½ teaspoon (2.5 grams) of kosher salt and ¼ teaspoon (0.75 grams) of black pepper and stir to combine.
2. Add the water, cover the potatoes, and cook for 6 minutes, occasionally stirring until tender. Remove the potatoes from the skillet, place them in a large bowl, and set them aside.
3. Add the sausage to the same skillet and cook it for 5 minutes, breaking it into smaller pieces with a wooden spoon until it is no longer pink.
4. In a medium bowl, whisk the eggs, whole milk, and the remaining kosher salt and black pepper until combined. Add it to the sausage and cook it for 2-3 minutes, often stirring until the eggs are scrambled.
5. Preheat the air fryer to 390°F (198°C) for 5 minutes.
6. Add the scrambled eggs mixture and cheddar cheese to the potatoes and mix until combined. Place the tortillas on your countertop, divide the filling between each tortilla, and roll each tortilla into a burrito.
7. Place the burritos in the air fryer seam-side down, then mist them lightly with avocado oil and bake them at 390°F (198°C) for 2 minutes. Flip the burritos over and cook them for 2 minutes until lightly golden.

Notes

- This recipe is designed to cook 1 burrito in a 4 L air fryer or 2 burritos in a 12 L air fryer basket-style air fryer.
- You can cook 3-4 burritos at the same time in a 16 L or an extra-large 25 L rack-style air fryer.

Tips

1. Warm the tortillas in the microwave or a dry skillet to make them easier to fold into a burrito.
2. Do not overfill the burritos, or the filling may ooze out as they cook in the air fryer.

WARM SPICED VANILLA FRENCH TOAST STICKS

Prep Time
5 MINUTES

Cook Time
20 MINUTES

Total Time
25 MINUTES

Serves
4

INGREDIENTS

- 3 large eggs
- ½ cup (114 ml) coconut milk
- 1 teaspoon (3 grams) pumpkin pie spice
- 2 tablespoons (30 ml) maple syrup
- 1 teaspoon (5 ml) pure vanilla extract
- 6 slices brioche bread, cut into 1/2-inch (1.25 cm) pieces

NUTRITION INFO

SERVING SIZE: 6 FRENCH TOAST STICKS	
Calories	367 kcal
Carbohydrates	56 g
Fats	7.5 g
Protein	13.7 g
Sugar	7.7 g
Sodium	559 mg
Cholesterol	131 mg

INSTRUCTIONS

1. Preheat the air fryer to 375°F (190°C).

2. Meanwhile, whisk the eggs, coconut milk, pumpkin pie spice, maple syrup, and pure vanilla extract in a shallow baking dish until combined.

3. Line the basket with parchment paper, then dip 8-12 pieces of bread into the custard and place them in the basket, making sure not to overcrowd it.

4. Air fry the French toast sticks for 5-6 minutes until golden brown.

5. Place them on a plate and repeat steps 3-4 until all the French toast sticks have been cooked.

6. Serve with maple syrup or fresh fruit if desired.

Notes

- This recipe is designed for a 12 L air fryer basket-style air fryer.

- If you want to cook them in a 4 L basket-style air fryer, cook 3-4 French toast sticks at a time.

- If you are using a 16 L or 25 L rack-style oven, you may be able to cook more French toast sticks at the same time. However, you may have to cook the French toast sticks for 3-5 minutes longer.

Tips

1. If you do not want to use brioche bread, use challah or whole-grain bread instead.

2. Use bread that is at least a day old to make the French toast sticks. If you use fresh bread, the French toast sticks may have a mushy texture.

3. Dip the bread in the custard. Do not soak it, or the bread will soak up too much moisture.

VEGGIE OVERLOAD BREAKFAST FRITTATA

Prep Time	Cook Time	Total Time	Serves
5 MINUTES	**20 MINUTES**	**25 MINUTES**	**2**

INGREDIENTS

- Olive oil, for misting
- 4 large eggs
- ½ teaspoon (3 grams) kosher salt
- ½ teaspoon (1.5 grams) black pepper
- 1 cup (125 grams) button mushrooms, diced finely
- 3 tablespoons (30 grams) red bell pepper, diced
- 2 shallots, diced
- 2 cloves garlic, diced
- 1 cup (30 grams) baby spinach, chopped
- ½ cup (50 grams) shredded Mexican cheese

INSTRUCTIONS

1. Preheat the air fryer to 360°F (182°C).
2. Lightly mist a nonstick 6-inch (15 cm) cake pan with olive oil.
3. Whisk the eggs, kosher salt, and black pepper in a large bowl until combined.
4. Add the mushrooms, red bell pepper, shallots, garlic, spinach, and Mexican cheese and whisk until combined.
5. Pour it into the prepared pan, then place the pan in the air fryer. Bake it for 18-20 minutes until the eggs are set.

Notes

- This frittata can be cooked in any basket or rack-style air fryer that is large enough to fit a 6-inch (15 cm) pan.

Tips

1. If you want the veggies to have a softer texture, sauté them for 3-5 minutes in a large skillet on the stove until they soften before adding them to the frittata batter. However, you will have to let them cool slightly before adding them to the batter to prevent the eggs from scrambling.
2. If frittata is browning too much, cover it with foil to prevent it from browning further.

NUTRITION INFO

SERVING SIZE: 1/2 A FRITTATA

Calories	287 kcal
Carbohydrates	17.6 g
Fats	16 g
Protein	22.1 g
Sugar	6 g
Sodium	643 mg
Cholesterol	372 mg

FLAKY SAUSAGE EGG POUCHES

Prep Time
10 MINUTES

Cook Time
18 MINUTES

Total Time
28 MINUTES

Serves
6

INGREDIENTS

- ¼ lb. (113 grams) pork Italian sausage
- 5 large eggs
- 2 tablespoons (20 grams) white onion, minced
- 2 tablespoons (20 grams) green bell pepper, minced
- 1 garlic clove, minced
- 1 17.3 oz. (0.5 kg) box puff pastry sheets
- ½ cup (50 grams) shredded cheddar cheese

NUTRITION INFO

SERVING SIZE: 1 BREAKFAST POCKET	
Calories	159 kcal
Carbohydrates	10.5 g
Fats	9.9 g
Protein	7.8 g
Sugar	1.8 g
Sodium	238 mg
Cholesterol	163 mg

INSTRUCTIONS

1. Place the Italian sausage in a medium non-stick skillet, set it over medium-high heat, and cook it for 5 minutes, breaking it into smaller pieces with a wooden spoon until it is no longer pink.

2. Whisk the eggs in a large bowl until combined. Add the white onion, green bell pepper, and garlic and mix until combined. Add it to the sausage and cook it for 2-3 minutes, often stirring until the eggs are scrambled. Remove it from the heat and set it aside.

3. Preheat the air fryer to 370°F (187°C) for 5 minutes.

4. Place the puff pastry on your countertop and cut the pastry into twelve 4-inch (10 cm) squares with a pizza cutter or knife.

5. Spoon the eggs and sausage filling in the center of 6 of the puff pastries, then top with cheddar cheese. Place the other 6 puff pastry squares on top of the filling. Press the edges of the puff pastry with a fork to seal them.

6. Place the breakfast pockets in the air fryer basket and bake them at 370°F (187°C) for 8-10 minutes until golden brown.

Notes

- This recipe is designed for a 16 L or 25 L rack-style air fryer.
- You can cook the breakfast pockets in a 4 L or 16 L basket-style air fryer in batches of 2-4.

Tips

1. Use cold puff pastry. The butter in the puff pastry melts as the breakfast pockets bake in the air fryer, creating flaky layers.

2. Do not overfill the breakfast pockets, or the filling will come out of the pastry.

EGGSCELLENT SCOTCH BITES

Prep Time	Cook Time	Total Time	Serves
15 MINUTES	**15 MINUTES**	**30 MINUTES**	**3**

INGREDIENTS

Dipping Sauce

- 3 tablespoons (53 grams) of plain, non-fat Greek yogurt
- 1 tablespoon (15 grams) Dijon mustard
- 1 tablespoon (15 grams) mayonnaise
- ⅛ teaspoon (0.5 grams) kosher salt
- ⅛ teaspoon (0.5 grams) cayenne pepper
- ⅛ teaspoon (0.5 grams) black pepper
- ⅛ teaspoon (0.5 grams) curry powder

Scotch Eggs

- 1 lb. (453 grams) pork sausage
- 6 hard-boiled eggs
- ⅓ cup (70 grams) wholewheat flour
- 2 large eggs
- 1 cup (119 grams) wholewheat panko bread crumbs
- Avocado oil for misting

INSTRUCTIONS

Dipping Sauce

1. Whisk the Greek yogurt, Dijon mustard, mayonnaise, kosher salt, cayenne pepper, black pepper, and curry powder in a small bowl combined. Cover the sauce with plastic wrap. Refrigerate until ready to serve.

Scotch Eggs

1. Divide the sausage into 6 uniform balls. Flatten each ball into a patty, then place 1 hard-boiled egg in the center of each patty.

2. Wrap the sausage around the hard-boiled eggs, making sure to seal all sides. Set them aside.

3. Preheat the air fryer to 390°F (198°C).

4. Meanwhile, place the flour into a small bowl. Place the 2 uncooked eggs in a small bowl and whisk until combined. Place the panko breadcrumbs into a shallow baking dish.

5. Dredge the Scotch eggs into the flour, then into the eggs, allowing the excess eggs to drip off. Roll them in the panko breadcrumbs, then place them onto a plate.

6. Coat the air fryer basket lightly with avocado oil. Place the Scotch eggs in the basket in an even layer and air fry them for 6 minutes. Flip them over and cook them for another 6 minutes until golden brown.

7. Serve with the dipping sauce.

NUTRITION INFO

SERVING SIZE: 2 SCOTCH EGGS

Calories	452 kcal
Carbohydrates	18.8 g
Fats	28.3 g
Protein	30.5 g
Sugar	10.3 g
Sodium	662 mg
Cholesterol	639 mg

Notes

- This recipe is designed for a 12 L basket-style or 16 L rack-style air fryer.
- You can cook the scotch eggs in 2-3 batches in a 4 L basket-style air fryer or 1 batch in a 25 L rack-style air fryer.

Tips

1. Moisten your hands with water before wrapping the eggs with sausage. The sausage won't stick to your fingers as much.

2. Press the sausage around the egg firmly to seal it so there are no gaps between the egg and the meat.

SUNNY STUFFED BREAKFAST SPUDS

Prep Time	Cook Time	Total Time	Serves
10 MINUTES	18 MINUTES	28 MINUTES	4

INGREDIENTS

- 2 medium whole sweet potatoes, cooked
- 2 teaspoons (10 ml) olive oil
- 4 large eggs
- ¼ cup (60 ml) whole milk
- ½ teaspoon (3 grams) kosher salt
- ½ teaspoon (3 grams) black pepper
- ⅓ cup (75 grams) shredded cheddar cheese
- 4 slices of cooked bacon, crumbled
- ½ cup (114 grams) cherry tomatoes, sliced thinly
- 2 green onions, sliced

NUTRITION INFO
SERVING SIZE:
1 SWEET POTATO SKIN

Calories	285 kcal
Carbohydrates	19.5 g
Fats	17.4 g
Protein	13.3 g
Sugar	5.4 g
Sodium	418 mg
Cholesterol	199 mg

INSTRUCTIONS

1. Preheat the air fryer to 400°F (204°C).

2. Cut the sweet potatoes in half and remove the flesh, leaving a ¼ inch (6 mm) border around the edges.

3. Place the sweet potatoes on a plate, brush them with olive oil, and place them in the air fryer. Roast at 400°F (204°C) for 10 minutes. Place the sweet potato skins on a plate.

4. Whisk the eggs, whole milk, kosher salt, and black pepper in a large bowl until combined.

5. Mist an air fryer cake pan with avocado oil and add the eggs. Bake for 3 minutes at 400°F (204°C) until the eggs are set. Scramble the eggs with a fork.

6. Divide the eggs between the potato skins and sprinkle them with cheddar cheese and bacon. Place the sweet potato skins back into the air fryer basket and cook them for 3-4 minutes until the cheese melts.

7. Place the sweet potato skins on a plate and top with cherry tomatoes, and green onions.

Notes

- This recipe is designed for a 12 L basket-style, 16 L rack-style air fryer, or 25 L rack-style air fryer.

- Cook the sweet potato skins in 2 batches if you are using a 4 L air fryer.

Tips

1. Do not scoop out all the sweet potato flesh. If you remove too much of the flesh, the skin will collapse.

2. Don't throw away the sweet potato flesh. Use it to make whipped sweet potatoes, sweet potato pie, biscuits, or a souffle.

MORNING EGG ROLL FIESTA

Prep Time	Cook Time	Total Time	Serves
10 MINUTES	20 MINUTES	30 MINUTES	6

INGREDIENTS

- ½ lb. (227 grams) Italian turkey sausage
- 6 large eggs
- 1 tablespoon (15 ml) water
- ¼ teaspoon (1.5 grams) kosher salt
- ¼ teaspoon (1.5 grams) black pepper
- 2 tablespoons (15 grams) green onions, chopped
- 2 tablespoons (20 grams) red bell pepper, diced
- 1 cup (85 grams) shredded potato hash browns
- 12 egg roll wrappers
- Water for the wrappers
- Olive oil spray

NUTRITION INFO

SERVING SIZE: 2 EGG ROLLS

Calories	349 kcal
Carbohydrates	60.8 g
Fats	5.2 g
Protein	18.1 g
Sugar	3.2 g
Sodium	649 mg
Cholesterol	181 mg

INSTRUCTIONS

1. Place the Italian turkey sausage in a medium non-stick skillet, set it over medium-high heat, and cook it for 5 minutes, breaking it into smaller pieces with a wooden spoon until it is no longer pink.

2. Whisk eggs, water, kosher salt, black pepper, green onions, and bell peppers in a medium bowl until combined. Add this egg and vegetable mixture to the sausage and cook it for 2-3 minutes, stirring often until the eggs are scrambled. Add the hash browns to the eggs, cook for 2 minutes, then remove it from the heat and set it aside.

3. Preheat the air fryer to 375°F (190°C).

4. Place 1 egg roll wrapper on your countertop. Place 1/4 cup (60 grams) of filling in the center of the wrapper. Wet the edges of the wrapper with a little water, then roll it into an eggroll. Place the egg roll on a plate. Repeat until you have 12 egg rolls.

5. Mist both sides of the egg rolls lightly with olive oil. Place egg rolls in the air fryer and air fry for 5 minutes at 375°F (190°C). Flip the egg rolls and cook them for another 5 minutes until golden.

Notes

- This recipe is designed for a 12 L basket-style, 16 L rack-style air fryer, or 25 L rack-style air fryer.
- Cook the egg rolls in 3-4 batches if you are using a 4 L air fryer.

Tips

1. When assembling the egg rolls, cover the wrappers you are not using with a clean, damp cloth. The cloth prevents them from drying out, making them easier to roll.

2. Keep the egg rolls warm in a 225°F (107°C) oven until ready to serve.

BLUEBERRY EUPHORIA SCONES

Prep Time
15 MINUTES

Cook Time
12 MINUTES

Total Time
17 MINUTES

Serves
8 SCONES

INGREDIENTS

Scones

- 1 ¾ cups (210 grams) whole wheat flour
- ¼ cup (50 grams) granulated sugar
- ¼ teaspoon (1.5 grams) fine sea salt
- 1 teaspoon (2 grams) fresh lemon zest
- 2 teaspoons (10 grams) baking powder
- ½ cup (1 stick or 120 grams) cold unsalted butter, cut into cubes
- 1 large egg
- ⅓ cup (80 ml) whole milk
- 1 teaspoon (5 ml) vanilla extract
- ¾ cup (142 grams) fresh blueberries
- 1 large egg yolk, for egg wash
- 1 tablespoon (15 ml) whole milk, for egg wash

Glaze

- 1 cup (120 grams) powdered sugar
- 1 tablespoon (15 ml) fresh lemon juice
- 1 tablespoon (15 ml) whole milk
- 1 teaspoon (5 ml) vanilla extract

INSTRUCTIONS

Blueberry Scones

1. Whisk the whole wheat flour, granulated sugar, fine sea salt, lemon zest, and baking powder in a large bowl until combined.
2. Add the butter. Use a pastry cutter, 2 knives, or clean hands to cut the butter into the flour until it looks like coarse crumbs.
3. Mix the egg, whole milk, and vanilla extract in a small bowl until combined, then make a well in the center of the dry ingredients, add the egg mixture, and mix until a soft dough forms. Fold in the blueberries.
4. Preheat the air fryer to 350°F (176°C).
5. Dust your countertop lightly with flour, then turn the dough out on your countertop. Knead the dough until it is no longer sticky.
6. Press dough into a 1-inch (2.5 cm) thick circle, then cut it into 8 scones. Place the blueberry scones in the air fryer basket.
7. To make egg wash, whisk egg yolk and the remaining whole milk in a small bowl until combined. Brush the blueberry scones with the egg wash. Bake them for 10-12 minutes at 350°F (176°F) until golden brown.
8. Place the scones on a cooling rack and set them aside to cool slightly.

Glaze

1. In a small bowl, whisk powdered sugar, whole milk, vanilla extract, and lemon juice until a smooth glaze forms.
2. Drizzle it over the blueberry scones before serving.

NUTRITION INFO

SERVING SIZE: 1 SCONE

Calories	141 kcal
Carbohydrates	17.8 g
Fats	5.5 g
Protein	5.3 g
Sugar	11.3 g
Sodium	89 mg
Cholesterol	57 mg

Notes

- This recipe is designed for a 16 L rack-style air fryer or 25 L rack-style air fryer.
- You can cook the scones in a 4 L air fryer in 4 batches or in a 12 L air fryer in 2 batches.

Tips

1. Use extremely cold butter. Cut it into cubes, then chill it in the freezer for 10-15 minutes before making the scones.
2. Do not overmix the scone dough, or the scones will have a tough texture.

CHAPTER 2
POULTRY RECIPES

GOLDEN ROASTED CHICKEN THIGHS

Prep Time
5 MINUTES

Cook Time
25 MINUTES

Total Time
30 MINUTES

Serves
4

INGREDIENTS

- 4 bone-in, skin-on chicken thighs, trimmed
- 1 teaspoon (5 grams) kosher salt
- 1 teaspoon (2 grams) smoked paprika
- 1 teaspoon (5 grams) garlic powder
- ½ teaspoon (3 grams) dried oregano
- ½ teaspoon (0.5 grams) Italian seasoning
- ¼ teaspoon (1.5 grams) cayenne pepper
- ½ teaspoon (3 grams) onion powder
- Avocado oil, for misting

INSTRUCTIONS

1. Preheat the air fryer to 380°F (193°C).

2. Place the chicken thighs in a large bowl, add the kosher salt, smoked paprika, garlic powder, dried oregano, Italian seasoning, cayenne pepper, and onion powder, and toss to coat the chicken thighs in the seasonings.

3. Mist the basket or rack with avocado oil, add the chicken thighs to the basket, skin side down, and roast at 380°F (193°C) for 12 minutes.

4. Flip the chicken thighs and roast them for 10-15 minutes until they have an internal temperature of 165°F (73°C).

Notes

- This recipe is designed for a 12 L basket-style air fryer, 16 L rack-style air fryer, or 25 L rack-style air fryer.
- You can cook the chicken thighs in two batches in a 4 L basket-style air fryer.

Tips

1. For super crispy chicken thighs, cook them skin-side up for an additional 4-5 minutes.

2. Marinate the chicken thighs in the fridge for a few hours or overnight for more flavor.

NUTRITION INFO

SERVING SIZE: 1 CHICKEN THIGH

Calories	269 kcal
Carbohydrates	14.4 g
Fats	9.5 g
Protein	19.8 g
Sugar	2.6 g
Sodium	232 mg
Cholesterol	80 mg

THAI TANGO CHICKEN SATAY

Prep Time
10 MINUTES

Cook Time
20 MINUTES

Total Time
30 MINUTES

Serves
6

INGREDIENTS

Chicken Satay

- 1 lb. (453 grams) boneless skinless chicken thighs
- 1 teaspoon (5 grams) ground turmeric
- 1 teaspoon (5 grams) ground coriander
- ½ teaspoon (3 grams) white pepper
- ½ teaspoon (3 grams) ground cumin
- ¼ cup (60 ml) coconut milk
- 2 tablespoons (30 ml) low-sodium tamari
- 3 teaspoons (15 grams) grated ginger
- 2 cloves garlic, grated
- Zest of 1 lime
- Juice of 1 lime
- 1 tablespoon (15 ml) sriracha
- Avocado oil, for misting

Peanut Sauce

- 2 tablespoons (15 ml) red curry paste
- ¼ cup (60 grams) natural creamy peanut butter
- 2 tablespoons (15 ml) honey
- 2 teaspoons (10 ml) low-sodium tamari
- ¼ teaspoon (1.5 ml) kosher salt
- 1 tablespoon (15 ml) apple cider vinegar
- ¼ cup (60 ml) water
- ½ cup (120 ml) coconut milk
- 2 tablespoons (16 grams) roasted unsalted peanuts, crushed for garnish
- 1 teaspoon (3 grams) sesame seeds, for garnish

INSTRUCTIONS

1. Preheat the air fryer to 370°F (187°C).

2. Mix the chicken thighs, turmeric, coriander, white pepper, ground cumin, coconut milk, tamari, ginger, garlic, lime zest, lime juice, and sriracha in a large bowl until combined.

3. Mist the air fryer basket with avocado oil, place the chicken thighs in the basket in a single layer and roast them at 370°F (187°C) for 15 minutes.

4. Turn the chicken thighs over and cook them for another 8-10 minutes until they have an internal temperature of 165°F (73°C).

Peanut Sauce

1. While the chicken thighs are cooking, whisk the red curry paste, creamy peanut butter, honey, tamari, kosher salt, apple cider vinegar, water, and coconut milk in a small pot. Set it over medium-high heat, then let it come to a simmer. Decrease the heat to low and cook it for 5 minutes, stirring occasionally until it thickens slightly.

2. Garnish the chicken satay with crushed peanuts and sesame seeds and serve with peanut sauce.

NUTRITION INFO

SERVING SIZE: 1 CHICKEN THIGH + 1/4 CUP OF PEANUT SAUCE

Calories	297 kcal
Carbohydrates	17.2 g
Fats	12.8 g
Protein	28.8 g
Sugar	10.2 g
Sodium	736 mg
Cholesterol	73 mg

Notes

- This recipe is designed for a 12 L basket-style air fryer, 16 L rack-style air fryer, or 25 L rack-style air fryer.
- You can cook the chicken thighs in 2 batches in a 4 L basket-style air fryer.

Tips

1. Marinate the chicken thighs for 30 minutes or overnight in the fridge to increase their flavor.

2. If the peanut sauce is not thick enough, place it over a medium-low flame. Make a slurry by combining 2 teaspoons of cornstarch with a tablespoon of water in a small bowl until combined. Add it to the sauce, mix until combined, and let it cook for 2-3 minutes until it reaches your desired thickness.

DIVINE CHICKEN PARMESAN

Prep Time
10 MINUTES

Cook Time
10 MINUTES

Total Time
20 MINUTES

Serves
4

INGREDIENTS

- 8 oz. (100 grams) whole grain linguine
- 2 boneless, skinless chicken breasts, trimmed, cut in half horizontally
- ¼ cup (60 grams) shredded Parmesan cheese
- 1 cup (119 grams) whole wheat Italian-style bread crumbs
- 2 tablespoons (8 grams) fresh parsley, minced
- 1 teaspoon (5 grams) garlic powder
- 2 large eggs
- ½ cup (112 grams) marinara sauce
- ½ cup (112 grams) mozzarella cheese
- 1 ½ cups (336 grams) warm marinara sauce

NUTRITION INFO

SERVING SIZE: 1 CHICKEN PARMESAN + 4 OZ. LINGUINE

Calories	351 kcal
Carbohydrates	35.7 g
Fats	8.2 g
Protein	30.1 g
Sugar	4 g
Sodium	637 mg
Cholesterol	153 mg

INSTRUCTIONS

1. Cook the linguine in salted boiling water using the manufacturer's directions. Drain it and set it aside.

2. Preheat the air fryer to 360°F (182°C).

3. Meanwhile, mix the parmesan cheese, bread crumbs, parsley, and garlic powder in a shallow baking dish until combined.

4. Mix the eggs in a shallow baking dish until combined.

5. Dip the chicken breasts into the beaten eggs, then dredge them with the breadcrumb mixture and place them on a plate.

6. Place the chicken breasts in an air fryer pan in a single layer and air fry them for 6 minutes at 360°F (182°C). Flip the chicken breasts over, and top each one with 2 tablespoons (30 ml) of marinara sauce and 2 tablespoons (30 grams) of shredded mozzarella cheese. Air fry the chicken breasts for 3-4 minutes until the cheese melts and the chicken reaches an internal temperature of 165°F (73°C).

7. Toss the linguine with the warm marinara sauce, then divide it between 4 bowls. Top with the chicken parmesan and extra warm marinara sauce if desired.

Notes

- This recipe is designed for a 16 L rack-style air fryer or 25 L rack-style air fryer.

- You can cook the chicken parmesan in 2 batches in a 4 L basket-style air fryer or a 16 L basket-style air fryer.

Tips

1. If the chicken breasts are not the same thickness, pound them out with a meat mallet or rolling pin until they are uniform in thickness. This will help the chicken cook evenly.

2. If you are cooking the chicken parmesan in batches, keep the first batch warm in a 225°F (107°C) oven until you are ready to serve it.

SMOKY GARLIC CHICKEN WINGS

Prep Time
5 MINUTES

Cook Time
16 MINUTES

Total Time
21 MINUTES

Serves
4

INGREDIENTS

- 1 lb. (453 grams) chicken wings, cut into flats and drumsticks
- 1 tablespoon (15 ml) olive oil
- 1 tablespoon (10 grams) garlic powder
- 2 teaspoons (4 grams) smoked paprika
- ¼ teaspoon (1.5 grams) cayenne pepper
- 1 teaspoon (3 grams) onion powder
- ¼ teaspoon (1.5 grams) chili powder
- 2 teaspoons (6 grams) kosher salt

INSTRUCTIONS

1. Preheat the air fryer to 375°F (190°C).
2. Place the chicken wings into a large Ziplock bag, then add the olive oil. Toss to coat the wings in the oil.
3. Sprinkle the garlic powder, smoked paprika, cayenne pepper, onion powder, chili powder, and kosher salt over the chicken wings, then toss to coat them in the seasonings.
4. Arrange the chicken wings in the basket or on the rack, leaving space between each wing.
5. Air fry at 400°F (204°C) for 8 minutes. Flip them over and air fry for another 8 minutes until golden and crispy. Serve with your desired sauce.

Notes

- This recipe is designed for a 16 L rack-style air fryer or 25 L rack-style air fryer.
- You can cook the chicken wings in 3-4 batches in a 4 L basket-style air fryer or 2-3 batches in a 16 L basket-style air fryer.

Tips

1. Cut the wing tips off to prevent them from burning.
2. Dry the wings thoroughly. Excess moisture can prevent them from developing a crispy texture.
3. If you want really crispy wings, increase the temperature to 400°F (204°C) during the last 3-5 minutes of cooking time.

NUTRITION INFO

SERVING SIZE: 4 CHICKEN WINGS

Calories	80 kcal
Carbohydrates	0 g
Fats	7.5 g
Protein	4.8 g
Sugar	0 g
Sodium	159 mg
Cholesterol	19 mg

7-SPICE FRIED CHICKEN

Prep Time
5 MINUTES

Cook Time
25 MINUTES

Total Time
30 MINUTES

Serves
4

INGREDIENTS

- 1 cup (135 grams) whole wheat flour
- 1 teaspoon (3 grams) garlic powder
- 1 teaspoon (3 grams) onion powder
- 1/2 teaspoon (1.5 grams) celery salt
- 1 teaspoon (5 grams) kosher salt
- 1 1/2 teaspoons (3.5 grams) paprika
- 1/2 teaspoon (1.5 grams) ground oregano
- 1/2 teaspoon (1.5 grams) black pepper
- 1 large egg
- 4 bone-in skin-on chicken thighs
- Avocado oil for misting

INSTRUCTIONS

1. Preheat the air fryer to 390°F (198°C).

2. Place the whole wheat flour, garlic powder, onion powder, celery salt, kosher salt, paprika, oregano, and black pepper in a Ziplock bag. Shake to combine.

3. Whisk the egg in a small bowl.

4. Place the chicken thighs in the bag and shake to coat the chicken in the seasoned flour.

5. Next, dip each chicken thigh in the egg. Place the chicken thighs back into the flour and shake the bag to coat the chicken in the flour again.

6. Mist the air fryer basket with avocado oil, then add the chicken thighs skin-side down in an even layer.

7. Air fry them at 390°F (198°C) for 15 minutes, then flip them over, mix them lightly with avocado oil, and cook them for another 10 minutes until golden and crispy until they have an internal temperature of 165°F (73°C).

Notes

- This recipe is designed for a 12 L basket-style air fryer, 16 L rack-style air fryer, or 25 L rack-style air fryer.

- You can cook the chicken thighs 2 at a time in a 4 L basket-style air fryer.

Tips

1. Dry the chicken thoroughly with paper towels for extra crispy fried chicken.

2. Line the basket with parchment paper once it's preheated and before adding the chicken thighs for easy cleanup.

NUTRITION INFO

SERVING SIZE: 1 CHICKEN THIGH

Calories	228 kcal
Carbohydrates	7.3 g
Fats	21.2 g
Protein	19.6 g
Sugar	0 g
Sodium	173 mg
Cholesterol	142 mg

HONEY GARLIC CHICKEN DRUMSTICKS

Prep Time
5 MINUTES

Cook Time
20 MINUTES

Total Time
25 MINUTES

Serves
4

INGREDIENTS

- ⅓ cup (85 ml) honey
- ¼ cup (60 ml) low-sodium tamari
- 3 cloves garlic, grated
- 1 shallot, grated
- 1 teaspoon grated ginger
- ½ teaspoon (1.5 grams) white pepper
- 1 ½ teaspoons (7 grams) avocado oil
- 8 chicken drumsticks

NUTRITION INFO

SERVING SIZE: 2 CHICKEN DRUMSTICKS	
Calories	368 kcal
Carbohydrates	10 g
Fats	19.3 g
Protein	35.6 g
Sugar	7.4 g
Sodium	838 mg
Cholesterol	180 mg

INSTRUCTIONS

1. Preheat the air fryer to 350°F (176°C).

2. Mix the honey, tamari, garlic, shallots, ginger, white pepper, and avocado oil in a large bowl until combined. Remove 2 tablespoons (28 grams) of the marinade, place it in a small bowl, and set it aside.

3. Add the drumsticks and toss to coat the drumsticks in the marinade. Set them aside.

4. Arrange the chicken drumsticks in the air fryer basket. Leave some space between each drumstick. Air fry them at 350°F (176°C) for 5 minutes.

5. Brush the chicken drumsticks with half of the reserved marinade. Flip them over and brush them with the remaining marinade. Air fry the chicken drumsticks for another 10 minutes until they have an internal temperature of 165°F (73°C).

Notes

- This recipe is designed for a 16 L rack-style air fryer or 25 L rack-style air fryer.

- You can cook the chicken thighs in 4 batches in a 4 L air fryer or 2 batches in a 12 L air fryer.

Tips

1. Choose chicken drumsticks that are roughly the same size so they cook evenly.

2. Marinate the chicken drumsticks for 30 minutes or overnight in the fridge for a stronger honey-garlic flavor.

3. Do not increase the air fryer's temperature when cooking the chicken drumsticks. The marinade contains honey, which can burn easily at high temperatures.

SIZZLING SUNSET CHICKEN FAJITAS

Prep Time	Cook Time	Total Time	Serves
5 MINUTES	15 MINUTES	20 MINUTES	4

INGREDIENTS

- 4 boneless, skinless chicken breasts cut into ½-inch (1.25cm) strips
- 1 medium red bell pepper, cut into ½-inch (1.25cm) slices
- 1 medium yellow bell pepper, cut into ½-inch (1.25cm) slices
- 1 medium green bell pepper cut into ½-inch (1.25cm) slices
- 1 tablespoon (15 ml) avocado oil
- 2 teaspoons (5 grams) chili powder
- 1 teaspoon (5 grams) garlic powder
- ½ teaspoon (3 grams) onion powder
- 1 ½ teaspoons (3 grams) smoked paprika
- ¼ teaspoon (1.5 grams) cayenne pepper
- ¼ teaspoon (1.5 grams) black pepper
- 1 teaspoon (5 grams) kosher salt
- ½ teaspoon (1 gram) dried oregano
- 8 6-inch (15cm) whole wheat tortillas, warm, for serving
- ½ cup (75 grams) guacamole, for serving
- ½ cup (123 grams) sour cream, for serving
- ½ cup (128 grams) pico de gallo, for serving

INSTRUCTIONS

1. Preheat the air fryer to 390°F (198°F).
2. Place the chicken and bell peppers into a large bowl. Add the avocado oil and toss to combine.
3. Add chili powder, garlic powder, onion powder, smoked paprika, cayenne pepper, black pepper, kosher salt, and dried oregano to the chicken and vegetables and toss to coat them in the seasonings.
4. Place the chicken and vegetables in the air fryer and cook at 390°F (198°C) for 7 minutes. Flip them over and cook them for another 8 minutes.
5. Serve the chicken fajitas with warm tortillas, avocado, guacamole, sour cream, and pico de gallo.

NUTRITION INFO

SERVING SIZE: 1 CUP OF CHICKEN FAJITAS + 2 TORTILLAS & 2 TABLESPOONS (30 GRAMS) OF TOPPINGS

Calories	434 kcal
Carbohydrates	23.7 g
Fats	23.8 g
Protein	33.8 g
Sugar	5.1 g
Sodium	384 mg
Cholesterol	69 mg

Notes

- This recipe is designed for a 16 L rack-style air fryer or 25 L rack-style air fryer.
- You can cook the chicken fajitas in 3-4 batches in a 4 L basket-style air fryer or in 2 batches in a 12 L basket-style air fryer.

Tips

1. Cut the chicken breasts into uniform pieces so they cook evenly.
2. Marinate the chicken and vegetables for 30 minutes to increase their flavor.

ENCHANTED CHICKEN ENCHILADAS

Prep Time
8 MINUTES

Cook Time
22 MINUTES

Total Time
30 MINUTES

Serves
5

INGREDIENTS

- 2 boneless, skinless chicken breasts, cut into thin strips
- 1 tablespoon (15 ml) olive oil
- 2 teaspoons (28 grams) taco seasoning
- Olive oil for misting
- 10 x 6-inch (15 cm) whole wheat flour tortillas
- 1 x 28 oz can (793 grams) red enchilada sauce
- 1 x 15 oz can (425 grams) black beans, drained, rinsed
- 2 cups (222 grams) shredded Mexican cheese
- 1 small tomato, diced
- 2 tablespoons (31.6 grams) sour cream
- 2 tablespoons (6 grams) cilantro, chopped finely

NUTRITION INFO

SERVING SIZE: 2 ENCHILADAS

Calories	334 kcal
Carbohydrates	32.9 g
Fats	11 g
Protein	35.1 g
Sugar	3.4 g
Sodium	192 mg
Cholesterol	44 mg

INSTRUCTIONS

1. Place the chicken breasts into a large bowl. Add olive oil and toss to combine. Add taco seasoning and toss to coat the chicken breasts in the seasoning.
2. Place a medium non-stick skillet over medium-high heat. Add the chicken breast once the skillet is hot and cook for 5 minutes per side. Remove the chicken breast from the skillet, place it on a plate, then let it cool slightly.
3. Shred the chicken into small pieces and set it aside.
4. Preheat the air fryer to 390°F (198°C) for 5 minutes.
5. Put 1/2 cup (120 grams) of enchilada sauce in an air fryer cake pan and spread it into an even layer. Set it aside.
6. Arrange the tortillas on your countertop, and add 2 tablespoons (30 grams) of enchilada sauce to each tortilla. Add 1/4 cup (70 grams) of chicken breast, 1/4 cup (45 grams) of black beans, and 2 tablespoons (30 grams) of Mexican cheese.
7. Roll the tortillas into enchiladas and arrange them in an even layer in the air fryer cake pan.
8. Add the remaining enchilada sauce on top and spread it into an even layer, then sprinkle the remaining Mexican cheese on top.
9. Bake the enchiladas for 10 minutes at 350°F (176°C) until the cheese melts.
10. Sprinkle the tomatoes on top of the enchiladas, then drizzle the sour cream on top and garnish with cilantro.

Notes

- This recipe is designed for a 12 L basket-style air fryer, 16 L rack-style air fryer, or 25 L rack-style air fryer.
- You can cook the chicken enchiladas in 2 small 6-inch (15cm) cake pans in a 4 L basket-style air fryer in 2 batches.

Tips

1. Place the enchiladas in the cake pan, seam side down, to keep them from unraveling.
2. Do not submerge the enchiladas in the sauce, or they will have a soggy texture.

TOKYO NIGHTS CHICKEN YAKITORI

Prep Time	Cook Time	Total Time	Serves
10 MINUTES	**16 MINUTES**	**26 MINUTES**	**6**

INGREDIENTS

- ½ cup (125 ml) mirin
- ½ cup (125 ml) sake
- ½ cup (125 ml) low-sodium tamari
- 2 tablespoons (30 grams) brown sugar
- 2 cloves garlic, grated
- 2 teaspoons (4 grams) grated ginger
- 2 medium red bell peppers, cut into 2-inch (5 cm) pieces
- 6 large green onions, cut into 2-inch (5 cm) pieces
- 2 lbs. (906 grams) boneless skinless chicken thighs, cut into 1 ½ inch (4 cm) pieces
- 1 medium green onion, green parts only, sliced thinly
- 8 metal or wooden skewers soaked in water

INSTRUCTIONS

1. Preheat the air fryer to 390°F (198°C).
2. Place the mirin, sake, low-sodium tamari, brown sugar, garlic, and ginger in a small pot and stir until combined. Set it over medium-high heat. Let it come to a boil, then cook it for 2 minutes and remove it from the heat. Reserve half of the sauce and set it aside.
3. Thread the bell peppers, green onions, and chicken thighs onto 8 metal or wooden skewers soaked in water.
4. Place the chicken yakitori into an air fryer cake pan and air fry them at 390°F (198°C) for 5 minutes. Baste the chicken yakitori with sauce, then flip them over and baste them again.
5. Grill them for 7 minutes, basting the chicken yakitori with sauce every 2 minutes until fully cooked.
6. Garnish with green onions, then serve with the reserved sauce.

Notes

- This recipe is designed for a 12 L basket-style air fryer, 16 L rack-style air fryer, or 25 L rack-style air fryer.
- You can cook the chicken yakitori in 2-3 batches in a 4 L basket-style air fryer.

Tips

1. If using wooden skewers to make the chicken yakitori, soak in water for at least 30 minutes.
2. If there is any leftover basting sauce, discard it to prevent cross-contamination. Only serve the chicken yakitori with the reserved sauce.

NUTRITION INFO

SERVING SIZE: 2 SKEWERS

Calories	108 kcal
Carbohydrates	10 g
Fats	1.3 g
Protein	8.1 g
Sugar	4.6 g
Sodium	455 mg
Cholesterol	28 mg

ZESTY LEMON PEPPER TURKEY WINGS

Prep Time	Cook Time	Total Time	Serves
5 MINUTES	25 MINUTES	30 MINUTES	6

INGREDIENTS

Turkey Wings

- 2 ½ lbs. (1133 grams) turkey wings
- 2 (6 grams) teaspoons lemon pepper
- 1 tablespoon (15 ml) avocado oil
- 2 teaspoons (5 grams) dried parsley
- ½ teaspoon (5 grams) kosher salt
- 1 teaspoon (5 grams) onion powder
- 1 teaspoon (5 grams) garlic powder
- ½ teaspoon (2 grams) dried thyme
- Juice of ½ lemon

Lemon Butter Sauce

- 4 tablespoons (60 grams) butter
- Juice of ½ lemon
- 4 garlic cloves, minced
- 1 shallot, minced
- 1 teaspoon (3 grams) lemon pepper
- 2 tablespoons (8 grams) fresh parsley

INSTRUCTIONS

Turkey Wings

1. Preheat the air fryer to 350°F (176°C).
2. Place turkey wings in a large bowl. Add lemon pepper, avocado oil, dried parsley, kosher salt, onion powder, garlic powder, thyme, and lemon juice and toss to coat the wings in the seasonings.
3. Add the wings to the basket or rack. Bake them at 350°F (176°C) for 10 minutes. Flip them over and bake for another 15 minutes until they reach an internal temperature of 165°F (73°C).

Lemon Butter Sauce

1. Meanwhile, place the butter into a small bowl and melt it in the microwave.
2. Add the lemon juice, garlic, shallot, lemon pepper, and parsley and mix until combined.
3. Place the cooked turkey wings in a large bowl, pour the lemon butter sauce on top, and toss to combine.

NUTRITION INFO

SERVING SIZE: 2 TURKEY WINGS

Calories	175 kcal
Carbohydrates	3 g
Fats	13.9 g
Protein	10.5 g
Sugar	0.9 g
Sodium	136 mg
Cholesterol	20 mg

Notes

- This recipe is designed for a 12 L basket-style air fryer, 16 L rack-style air fryer, or 25 L rack-style air fryer.
- You can cook the turkey wings in a 4 L basket-style air fryer in 3-4 batches.

Tips

1. Cut the tips off the turkey wings so they do not burn in the air fryer.
2. Let the turkey wings marinate in the fridge for 30 minutes or overnight for better flavor.
3. Let the turkey wings rest for 5-10 minutes before serving.

GOBBLE GOBBLE TURKEY MEATBALLS

Prep Time
5 MINUTES

Cook Time
20 MINUTES

Total Time
25 MINUTES

Serves
4

INGREDIENTS

- 1 lb. (453 grams) ground turkey
- ½ cup (60 grams) whole wheat Panko bread crumbs
- 1 large egg
- ¼ cup (15 grams) fresh parsley
- ¼ cup (25 grams) grated parmesan cheese
- ½ small white onion, minced
- 2 cloves garlic minced
- 1 tablespoon (15 ml) low-sodium tamari
- ½ teaspoon (1.5 grams) black pepper
- Avocado oil, for misting

INSTRUCTIONS

1. Preheat the air fryer to 400°F (204°C).
2. Mix all the ingredients in a bowl. Roll it into 1-inch (2.5 cm) meatballs and place them on a plate.
3. Mist the air fryer basket with avocado oil and add half of the meatballs to the basket.
4. Cook the meatballs for 5 minutes at 400°F (204°C), then flip them over and cook them for another 5 minutes until cooked through.
5. Repeat steps 3-4 to cook the remaining meatballs.

Notes

- This recipe is designed for a 12 L basket-style air fryer, 16 L rack-style air fryer, or 25 L rack-style air fryer.
- You can cook the meatballs in 3-4 batches in a 4 L basket-style air fryer.

Tips

1. Do not over-mix the meatball mixture, or the meatballs will be tough.
2. Scoop the meatballs with a 2-tablespoon (30 gram) cookie scoop to create more evenly sized meatballs or if you don't want to touch the meat with your hands.

NUTRITION INFO

SERVING SIZE: 6 MEATBALLS

Calories	113 kcal
Carbohydrates	4.2 g
Fats	5.3 g
Protein	12.6 g
Sugar	0.9 g
Sodium	325 mg
Cholesterol	54 mg

MEDITERRANEAN STYLE TURKEY BURGERS

Prep Time	Cook Time	Total Time	Serves
5 MINUTES	**12 MINUTES**	**17 MINUTES**	**4**

INGREDIENTS

- 1 lb. (454 grams) ground turkey
- ½ (1.5 grams) teaspoon black pepper
- 4 oz. (60 grams) crumbled feta cheese
- 1 cup (30 grams) spinach, packed finely chopped
- 2 tablespoons (30 grams) red onion, minced
- 2 tablespoons (30 grams) sun-dried tomatoes, minced
- ½ teaspoon (2 grams) garlic powder
- 1 teaspoon (5 ml) Worcestershire sauce
- 4 slices cheddar cheese
- 1 medium Roma tomato sliced
- 8 Romaine lettuce leaves
- 4 wholewheat burger buns

INSTRUCTIONS

1. Preheat the air fryer to 350°F (176°C).

2. Mix all the ingredients except the avocado oil in a bowl until combined. Shape it into 4 patties and place them on a plate.

3. Mist the air fryer basket lightly with avocado oil, then add the patties to the basket and air fry them for 6 minutes at 350°F (176°C). Flip them over and cook them for another 5 minutes until cooked through.

4. Add a slice of cheese to each patty, then cook them for 1 minute until it starts to melt.

5. Let them rest for 5 minutes. Place the bottom burger buns on 4 plates, add the burger patties, tomato, cheese, and your desired condiments, then add the top buns and serve.

Notes

- This recipe is designed for a 16 L rack-style air fryer or 25 L rack-style air fryer.

- You can cook the burgers two at a time in a 12 L basket-style air fryer or 4 L basket-style air fryer.

Tips

1. Wet your hands with water when shaping the turkey mixture into patties to prevent the meat from sticking to your hands.

2. Push your finger in the center of each turkey patty to make a slight indentation. This will keep the burgers from shrinking too much.

NUTRITION INFO

SERVING SIZE: 1 BURGER

Calories	411 kcal
Carbohydrates	57.2 g
Fats	13.3 g
Protein	23.3 g
Sugar	14.9 g
Sodium	635 mg
Cholesterol	23 mg

CAJUN TURKEY TENDERLOIN WITH MAPLE GLAZE

Prep Time
5 MINUTES

Cook Time
25 MINUTES

Total Time
30 MINUTES

Serves
4

INGREDIENTS

Turkey

- 1 ½ tablespoons (10 grams) smoked paprika
- 1 ½ teaspoons (2.5 grams) garlic powder
- 1 teaspoon (5 grams) kosher salt
- ½ teaspoon (3 grams) black pepper
- 1 teaspoon (5 grams) onion powder
- ½ teaspoon (3 grams) dried oregano
- 2 turkey breast tenderloins (1 lb./650 grams each)
- 1 tablespoon (15 ml) olive oil

Maple Glaze

- ⅓ cup (80 ml) chicken broth
- ¼ cup (60 ml) maple syrup
- 1 tablespoon (15 ml) low-sodium tamari
- 2 tablespoons (30 grams) brown sugar

NUTRITION INFO

SERVING SIZE: ½ TURKEY TENDERLOIN

Calories	108 kcal
Carbohydrates	5.9 g
Fats	4.2 g
Protein	13.2 g
Sugar	3.4 g
Sodium	323 mg
Cholesterol	20 mg

INSTRUCTIONS

Turkey

1. Preheat the air fryer to 400°F (204°C).
2. Mix the smoked paprika, garlic powder, kosher salt, black pepper, onion powder, and oregano in a small bowl until combined.
3. Brush both sides of each turkey tenderloin with olive oil, then sprinkle the seasoning blend all over the turkey tenderloins.
4. Place the turkey tenderloins in the air fryer basket and roast them at 400°F (204°C) for 10 minutes. Flip them over and roast them for 10-15 minutes until the tenderloins reach an internal temperature of 165°F (73°C). Let them rest for 5 minutes.

Maple Glaze

1. Meanwhile, place the chicken broth, maple syrup, low-sodium tamari, and brown sugar in a small pot. Place over medium-high heat and let it come to a boil.
2. Decrease the heat to low and cook it for 10-15 minutes until it reduces and thickens to a glaze.
3. Brush the turkey tenderloins with the glaze before serving.

Notes

- This recipe is designed for a 12 L basket-style air fryer, 16 L rack-style air fryer, or 25 L rack-style air fryer.
- You can cook the turkey tenderloins one at a time in a 4 L basket-style air fryer.

Tips

1. Marinate the turkey tenderloins with the Cajun seasoning for 30 minutes or 2-4 hours before air-frying them for better flavor.
2. If you want the maple glaze to have a thicker consistency, make a slurry by combining two teaspoons (5 grams) of cornstarch and one tablespoon of water. Whisk it into the glaze and cook it for 3-5 minutes until it reaches your desired consistency.

CHAPTER 3
BEEF & PORK RECIPES

SWEET AND SPICY MONGOLIAN BEEF

Prep Time
10 MINUTES

Cook Time
18 MINUTES

Total Time
28 MINUTES

Serves
4

INGREDIENTS

- 1 lb. (453 grams) flank steak, cut into 1/4-inch (6.5 mm) strips
- ¼ cup (30 grams) cornstarch
- Olive oil for misting
- 2 teaspoons (10 ml) olive oil
- 4 cloves garlic, minced
- 1 tablespoon (8 grams) minced ginger
- ½ cup (118 ml) low-sodium tamari
- ½ cup (118 ml) water
- ¼ cup (60 grams) brown sugar
- ¼ cup (60 ml) honey
- ½ teaspoon (3 grams) white pepper
- ½ teaspoon (3 grams) crushed red pepper flakes
- 2 small green onions, green parts only, thinly sliced
- 1 teaspoon (5 grams) sesame seeds

INSTRUCTIONS

1. Preheat the air fryer to 400°F (204°C).
2. Place the flank steak in a large bowl, add the cornstarch, and toss to combine. Let it sit for 5 minutes.
3. Mist the basket or rack with olive oil, add the flank steak, spread it into an even layer, and air fry at 400°F (204°C) for 5 minutes. Shake the basket or flip it over and air fry for another 5 minutes until tender.
4. Put the olive oil in a small pot and set it over medium-high heat. Add garlic and ginger. Cook for 30 seconds until fragrant.
5. Add tamari, water, brown sugar, honey, white pepper, and crushed red pepper flakes. Stir until combined. Let it come to a boil, then cook it for 6 minutes, occasionally stirring until it thickens.
6. Add the flank steak to the sauce, toss to combine, and cook it for 1-2 minutes. Garnish with green onions and sesame seeds.

Notes

- This recipe is designed for a 12 L basket-style air fryer, 16 L rack-style air fryer, or 25 L rack-style air fryer.
- You can cook the flank steak in two batches in a 4 L basket-style air fryer. Additionally, set the first batch aside until the second batch is done, then toss both batches in the sauce at the same time.

Tips

1. Cut the flank steak against the grain to make the beef more tender and reduce chewiness.
2. Put the flank steak in the freezer for 30 minutes before slicing. It will be easier to cut into uniform strips.

NUTRITION INFO

SERVING SIZE: 1 CUP (244 GRAMS) MONGOLIAN BEEF

Calories	191 kcal
Carbohydrates	19.1 g
Fats	9.7 g
Protein	7.3 g
Sugar	11.9 g
Sodium	131 mg
Cholesterol	18 mg

GOURMET PERFECTION FILET MIGNON

Prep Time
10 MINUTES

Cook Time
8 MINUTES

Total Time
18 MINUTES

Serves
2

INGREDIENTS

Garlic Herb Butter

- 2 tablespoons (30 grams) butter, softened
- 1 tablespoon (4 grams) fresh parsley, minced
- 1 clove garlic, minced
- 1 small shallot, minced

Filet Mignon

- ½ teaspoon (3 grams) onion powder
- 1 ½ (7 grams) teaspoons fine sea salt
- 1 teaspoon (5 grams) garlic powder
- 1 teaspoon (2 grams) paprika
- ½ teaspoon (3 grams) black pepper
- 1 teaspoon (5 grams) brown sugar
- 2 six oz. (340 grams) filet mignon steaks
- 2 tablespoons (15 ml) olive oil

INSTRUCTIONS

Garlic Herb Butter

1. Mix the butter, parsley, garlic, and shallot in a small bowl until combined. Set it aside.

Filet Mignon

1. Preheat the air fryer to 390°F (198°C).

2. In a small bowl, whisk onion powder, sea salt, garlic powder, paprika, black pepper, and brown sugar until combined.

3. Sprinkle it on both sides of each steak, patting the seasoning into the steaks.

4. Brush both sides of each steak with a tablespoon of olive oil, then add them to the air fryer and cook them for 4 minutes at 390°F (198°C).

5. Flip the steaks over and cook them for another 4 minutes until they reach your desired level of doneness.

6. Place the steak on two plates. Top each steak with a tablespoon of garlic butter, then let them sit for 5 minutes before serving.

NUTRITION INFO

SERVING SIZE: 1 STEAK

Calories	476 kcal
Carbohydrates	4.5 g
Fats	36 g
Protein	29.3 g
Sugar	0.5 g
Sodium	531 mg
Cholesterol	116 mg

Notes

- This recipe is designed for a 4 L basket-style air fryer, 12 L basket-style air fryer, 16 L rack-style air fryer, or 25 L rack-style air fryer.

Tips

1. Let the steaks come to room temperature before air frying them. They will cook more evenly.

2. Let the steaks marinate in the fridge overnight to allow the seasoning to penetrate deep into the meat.

3. Use ribeye, T-bone, or sirloin steak if you do not like filet mignon.

SUCCULENT BEEF AND BROCCOLI MEDLEY

Prep Time
5 MINUTES

Cook Time
25 MINUTES

Total Time
30 MINUTES

Serves
4

INGREDIENTS

- ⅓ cup (90 ml) low-sodium tamari
- ¼ cup (60 ml) water
- 2 tablespoons (15 ml) toasted sesame oil
- 1 teaspoon (5 ml) crushed red pepper flakes
- 3 cloves garlic, minced
- 1 shallot, minced
- 1 teaspoon (2 grams) grated ginger
- 1 lb. (453 grams) flank steak, thinly sliced
- 1 lb. (180 grams) broccoli florets
- 1 teaspoon (5 ml) olive oil
- ½ teaspoon (1.25 grams) cornstarch
- 1 teaspoon (5 grams) sesame seeds
- 2 tablespoons (11 grams) green onions, green parts only, sliced thinly

INSTRUCTIONS

1. Mix the tamari, water, sesame oil, crushed red pepper flakes, garlic, shallots, and ginger in a small bowl until combined.

2. Preheat the air fryer to 375°F (190°C).

3. Place the flank steak into a large bowl, pour half of the sauce over it, and toss to combine. Reserve the remaining sauce for later.

4. Place the steaks in the air fryer basket. Air fry the steaks for 8 minutes at 375°F (190°C).

5. Place the broccoli in a large bowl. Add olive oil, then toss to coat the broccoli in the olive oil. Add the broccoli to the air fryer and air fry for 5 minutes.

6. Add the cornstarch to the reserved sauce. Mix until combined. Heat the sauce in the microwave for a minute, then stir to combine, and heat it for another minute until it thickens.

7. Place the beef and broccoli in a large bowl. Add the sauce and toss to combine. Garnish with sesame seeds and green onions.

Notes

- This recipe is designed for a 12 L basket-style air fryer, 16 L rack-style air fryer, or 25 L rack-style air fryer.

- You can cook the beef and broccoli in 2 batches using a 4 L basket-style air fryer.

Tips

1. If the sauce is not thick enough to coat the back of a wooden spoon, add another ½ teaspoon (1.25 grams) of cornstarch, whisk until combined, and heat it for another minute in the microwave.

2. If the sauce is too thick, add a teaspoon (5 ml) of water, stir to combine, and heat it in the microwave for another minute.

NUTRITION INFO

SERVING SIZE: 1 CUP (217 GRAMS) OF BEEF AND BROCCOLI	
Calories	215 kcal
Carbohydrates	15.3 g
Fats	13.4 g
Protein	9.9 g
Sugar	1.4 g
Sodium	89 mg
Cholesterol	18 mg

BBQ CHEDDAR BURGERS

Prep Time	Cook Time	Total Time	Serves
10 MINUTES	12 MINUTES	22 MINUTES	4

INGREDIENTS

- 1 lb. (453 grams) 80/20 lean ground beef
- 1 teaspoon (5 grams) kosher salt
- ½ teaspoon (3 grams) black pepper
- ½ teaspoon (3 grams) onion powder
- 1 teaspoon (5 grams) garlic powder
- 1 teaspoon (2 grams) smoked paprika
- ¼ teaspoon (3 grams) cayenne pepper
- ¼ cup (30 grams) barbecue sauce
- 4 slices cheddar cheese
- 4 whole wheat hamburger buns
- Your preferred toppings

INSTRUCTIONS

1. Preheat the air fryer to 370°F (187°C).
2. Mix the ground beef, kosher salt, black pepper, onion powder, garlic powder, smoked paprika, and cayenne pepper in a large bowl until combined.
3. Divide it into 4 even portions and shape them into burger patties.
4. Brush both sides of the burgers with barbecue sauce, then add them to the air fryer and air fry for 6 minutes at 370°F (187°C). Flip them over and air fry for 3-5 minutes.
5. Place the burgers on a plate.
6. Add a parchment liner to the basket, then place the burgers back in the basket and add a slice of cheese on top of each burger. Air fry for 1 minute or until the cheese melts.
7. Add the burgers to the hamburger buns. Add your desired toppings and serve.

Notes

- This recipe is designed for a 12 L basket-style air fryer, 16 L rack-style air fryer, or 25 L rack-style air fryer.
- You can cook the burgers in 2 batches using a 4 L basket-style air fryer.

Tips

1. Press an indent in the center of each patty to prevent it from shrinking too much.
2. Do not over-mix the burger meat, or the burgers will be tough and chewy.

NUTRITION INFO

SERVING SIZE: 1 BURGER	
Calories	235 kcal
Carbohydrates	28.4 g
Fats	6.8 g
Protein	10.5 g
Sugar	5 g
Sodium	471 mg
Cholesterol	23 mg

SWEET CHILI BBQ MEATLOAF

Prep Time
5 MINUTES

Cook Time
25 MINUTES

Total Time
30 MINUTES

Serves
4

INGREDIENTS

- 1 lb. (453 grams) lean 80/20 ground beef
- ½ medium red bell pepper, minced
- ½ medium red onion, minced
- 2 cloves garlic, minced
- ⅓ cup (40 grams) whole wheat bread crumbs
- 2 tablespoons (30 ml) whole milk
- 2 tablespoons (11 grams) grated parmesan cheese
- 1 tablespoon (4 grams) fresh parsley chopped
- 1 large egg
- 1 teaspoon (5 grams) kosher salt
- ½ teaspoon (3 grams) black pepper
- 1 teaspoon (2 grams) Italian seasoning
- ¼ cup (30 grams) BBQ sauce
- ¼ cup (65 grams) sweet chili sauce

INSTRUCTIONS

1. Preheat the air fryer to 350°F (176°C).

2. Mix ground beef, red bell pepper, red onion, garlic, bread crumbs, whole milk, parmesan cheese, parsley, egg, kosher salt, black pepper, and Italian seasoning in a large bowl until combined.

3. Shape the meat mixture into loaves that are about 5 inches (12 cm) long and 2 inches (5 cm) wide.

4. Place the meatloaves in the air fryer and bake for 20 minutes at 350°F (176°C).

5. Mix the BBQ sauce and sweet chili sauce in a small bowl until combined. Brush the meatloaves with the sauce and bake for another 5 minutes until they have an internal temperature of 160°F (171°C).

NUTRITION INFO

SERVING SIZE: 1/2 MEATLOAF

Calories	172 kcal
Carbohydrates	12.9 g
Fats	9.2 g
Protein	9.5 g
Sugar	8.8 g
Sodium	298 mg
Cholesterol	68 mg

Notes

- This recipe is designed for a 12 L basket-style air fryer, 16 L rack-style air fryer, or 25 L rack-style air fryer.

- You can cook smaller meatloaves 1 at a time using a 4 L basket-style air fryer.

Tips

1. Mix the meatloaf mixture just until combined. Otherwise, it will be tough.

2. Let the meatloaves sit for 5 minutes before serving.

CARNIVORE'S DELIGHT BEEF KABOBS

Prep Time
5 MINUTES

Cook Time
10 MINUTES

Total Time
15 MINUTES

Serves
4

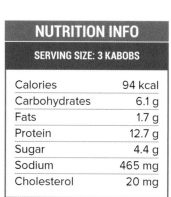

INGREDIENTS

- ½ cup (140 grams) plain Greek yogurt
- 2 tablespoons (30 ml) low-sodium tamari
- ½ teaspoon (3 grams) ground cumin
- 1 teaspoon (5 grams) kosher salt
- ¼ teaspoon (1.5 grams) black pepper
- 1 teaspoon (5 grams) chili powder
- 1 teaspoon (5 grams) light brown sugar
- 1 ½ lbs. (680 grams) sirloin steak, cut into 1-inch (2.5 cm) pieces
- 1 medium red bell pepper, cut into ½-inch (1.25 cm) pieces
- 1 medium yellow bell pepper, cut into ½-inch (1.25 cm) pieces
- 1 medium red onion, cut into ½-inch (1.25 cm) pieces
- 12 wooden or metal skewers

INSTRUCTIONS

1. Preheat the air fryer to 400°F (204°C).

2. In a large bowl, mix Greek yogurt, tamari, cumin, kosher salt, black pepper, chili powder, and brown sugar until combined.

3. Add the sirloin steak, red bell pepper, yellow bell pepper, and red onion. Toss to coat everything in the marinade.

4. Thread the sirloin, bell peppers, and red onions onto metal or wooden soaked skewers.

5. Place the beef kabobs in the air fryer and cook at 400°F (204°C) for 5 minutes. Flip the beef kabobs over and cook them for another 5 minutes.

NUTRITION INFO

SERVING SIZE: 3 KABOBS

Calories	94 kcal
Carbohydrates	6.1 g
Fats	1.7 g
Protein	12.7 g
Sugar	4.4 g
Sodium	465 mg
Cholesterol	20 mg

Notes

- This recipe is designed for a 12 L basket-style air fryer, 16 L rack-style air fryer, or 25 L rack-style air fryer.

- You can air fry the kabobs 3-4 at a time in a 4 L basket-style air fryer.

Tips

1. Let the sirloin steak sit out of the fridge for 30 minutes before air frying the kabobs to help them cook more evenly.

2. If using wooden skewers to make the beef kabobs, soak them in water for at least 30 minutes.

3. Most air fryers can only fit 6-8-inch (15-20 cm) skewers. If you use longer skewers, the kabobs won't fit in the air fryer.

OPA! ZEUS MEATBALLS

Prep Time
10 MINUTES

Cook Time
14 MINUTES

Total Time
24 MINUTES

Serves
4

INGREDIENTS

- ⅓ cup (40 grams) whole wheat breadcrumbs
- ½ medium red onion, minced
- 3 cloves garlic, minced
- 1 tablespoon (4 grams) fresh parsley, minced
- 1 tablespoon (2 grams) fresh mint, minced
- 1 teaspoon (5 grams) dried oregano
- 2 tablespoons (11 grams) grated parmesan cheese
- 2 teaspoons (6 grams) Greek seasoning
- ½ teaspoon (3 grams) black pepper
- 1 lb. (453 grams) lean ground beef
- ½ lb. (227 grams) lean ground pork

INSTRUCTIONS

1. Preheat the air fryer to 380°F (193°C).

2. Mix the breadcrumbs, red onion, garlic, parsley, mint, oregano, parmesan cheese, Greek seasoning, and black pepper in a large bowl until combined.

3. Add the ground beef and ground pork. Mix just until combined. Divide the mixture into 16 meatballs.

4. Add the meatballs to the air fryer and bake them for 12-14 minutes at 380°F (193°C) until they have a temperature of 165°F (73°C).

Notes

- This recipe is designed for a 16 L rack-style air fryer or 25 L rack-style air fryer.
- You can air fry the meatballs in 2 batches in a 12 L basket-style air fryer or in 3 batches in a 4 L basket-style air fryer.

Tips

1. Do not over-mix the meatball mixture.
2. Let the meatballs sit for 5 minutes before serving.

NUTRITION INFO

SERVING SIZE: 4 MEATBALLS

Calories	92 kcal
Carbohydrates	5 g
Fats	3.7 g
Protein	9.8 g
Sugar	2 g
Sodium	65 mg
Cholesterol	27 mg

SAVORY PORK CHOP PERFECTION

Prep Time
5 MINUTES

Cook Time
12 MINUTES

Total Time
17 MINUTES

Serves
2

INGREDIENTS

- 1 ½ teaspoons (7 grams) brown sugar
- 2 teaspoons (5 grams) smoked paprika
- 1 teaspoon (3 grams) herbs de Provence
- 1 ½ teaspoons (7 grams) kosher salt
- 1 teaspoon (5 grams) onion powder
- 1 teaspoon (5 grams) garlic powder
- 2 center-cut, bone-in pork chops
- 1 tablespoon (15 ml) olive oil

INSTRUCTIONS

1. Preheat the air fryer to 400°F (204°C).

2. In a small bowl, whisk brown sugar, smoked paprika, herbs de Provence, kosher salt, black pepper, onion powder, and garlic powder until combined.

3. Brush both sides of the pork chops with olive oil, then season them with the spice blend, making sure to massage the spice blend into the meat.

4. Place the pork chops in the air fryer and roast at 400°F (204°C) for 6 minutes. Flip pork chops and air fry them for another 6 minutes until they have an internal temperature of 145°F (63°C).

Notes

- This recipe is designed for a 4 L basket-style air fryer, 12 L basket-style air fryer, 16 L rack-style air fryer, or 25 L rack-style air fryer.

Tips

1. Pat pork chops dry with paper towels well, so the oil and seasonings stick.

2. Buy pork chops that are 1 ½ - 2 inches (4 - 5cm) thick. If the pork chops are any thinner than this, they will dry out easily.

NUTRITION INFO

SERVING SIZE: 1 PORK CHOP

Calories	243 kcal
Carbohydrates	4 g
Fats	15.9 g
Protein	20.4 g
Sugar	4 g
Sodium	265 mg
Cholesterol	71 mg

SIZZLING HARMONY BBQ RIBS

Prep Time
5 MINUTES

Cook Time
25 MINUTES

Total Time
30 MINUTES

Serves
4

INGREDIENTS

- 2 teaspoons (5 grams) smoked paprika
- 2 teaspoons (10 grams) brown sugar
- 1 teaspoon (5 grams) garlic powder
- 1 teaspoon (5 grams) onion powder
- ½ teaspoon (2 grams) chili powder
- ½ teaspoon (3 grams) black pepper
- 1 ½ teaspoons (7 grams) kosher salt
- 1 tablespoon (15 grams) mustard
- 2 ½ lbs. (1130 grams) rack of pork baby back ribs, membrane removed, cut in half
- 1 cup (240 grams) BBQ sauce

INSTRUCTIONS

1. Preheat the air fryer to 380°F (193°C).

2. Mix the smoked paprika, brown sugar, garlic powder, onion powder, chili powder, black pepper, and kosher salt in a small bowl until combined.

3. Rub the mustard over the baby's back ribs, then sprinkle the spice blend on both sides of the ribs. Massage the spices into the meat.

4. Place the ribs in the air fryer, meat side down, and bake them at 380°F (193°C) for 15 minutes.

5. Flip the ribs over and bake them for another 10 minutes until they have an internal temperature between 195°F (90°C) and 203°F (95°C).

6. Brush the ribs with BBQ sauce before serving.

Notes

- This recipe is designed for a 12 L basket-style air fryer, 16 L rack-style air fryer, or 25 L rack-style air fryer.

- You can air fry the ribs in a 4 L basket-style air fryer in 2 batches.

Tips

1. If you want the BBQ sauce to caramelize, return the ribs to the air fryer after you brush them with sauce. Air fry at 400°F (204°C) for 3-5 minutes until the sugars in the BBQ sauce caramelize.

2. You can also use this recipe to make spare ribs. However, they will take about 40 minutes to cook since they are a little thicker than baby back ribs.

NUTRITION INFO

SERVING SIZE: 1/2 RACK RIBS

Calories	339 kcal
Carbohydrates	19.9 g
Fats	22.1 g
Protein	16.2 g
Sugar	11.2 g
Sodium	486 mg
Cholesterol	50 mg

CHEESY SAUSAGE ZITI

Prep Time
10 MINUTES

Cook Time
20 MINUTES

Total Time
30 MINUTES

Serves
4

INGREDIENTS

- 4 oz. (113 grams) whole wheat penne pasta
- 1 tablespoon (15 ml) avocado oil
- 1 lb. (453 grams) ground Italian sausage
- ½ medium red onion, minced
- ½ medium red bell pepper, minced
- 2 cloves garlic, minced
- 1 teaspoon (2 grams) Italian seasoning
- ½ teaspoon (3 grams) dried basil
- 2 ½ cups (562 grams) marinara sauce
- ½ cup (45 grams) grated parmesan cheese
- 1 teaspoon (5 grams) kosher salt
- ½ teaspoon (3 grams) black pepper
- 1 cup (113 grams) shredded mozzarella cheese

INSTRUCTIONS

1. Cook penne pasta in salted boiling water using the manufacturer's directions. Drain it and place it in a large bowl.

2. Meanwhile, place the avocado oil in a large skillet and set it over medium-high heat.

3. Add Italian sausage to the pan. Cook it for 3 minutes, breaking it into small pieces.

4. Add the red onion, red bell pepper, garlic, Italian seasoning, and basil, and cook it for 4 minutes.

5. Add the marinara sauce, 1/4 cup (23 grams) of parmesan cheese, kosher salt, and black pepper and mix until combined. Cook everything for 7 minutes.

6. Preheat the air fryer to 350°F (176°C).

7. Add the sausage sauce to the penne pasta. Mix until combined. Pour it into an air fryer cake pan. Sprinkle the remaining parmesan and mozzarella cheese.

8. Place it in the air fryer and bake at 350°F (176°C) for 5-6 minutes until the cheese melts.

Notes

- This recipe is designed for a 12 L basket-style air fryer, 16 L rack-style air fryer, or 25 L rack-style air fryer.

- You can divide the ziti between two 6-inch (15 cm) pans and air fry them in a 4 L basket-style air fryer in 2 batches.

Tips

1. Cook the penne pasta until it's al dente. It continues cooking in the air fryer; if you fully cook the pasta, it will develop a mushy texture.

2. Use rigatoni, ziti, or any other short pasta you desire to make this recipe.

NUTRITION INFO

SERVING SIZE:
1 CUP (199 GRAMS) OF ZITI

Calories	462 kcal
Carbohydrates	93 g
Fats	9.4 g
Protein	17.9 g
Sugar	7.9 g
Sodium	747 mg
Cholesterol	8 mg

HONEY MUSTARD PORK TENDERLOIN

Prep Time	Cook Time	Total Time	Serves
5 MINUTES	25 MINUTES	30 MINUTES	4

INGREDIENTS

Pork Tenderloin

- 2 teaspoons (10 grams) brown sugar
- 1 teaspoon (2 teaspoons) smoked paprika
- 1 teaspoon (2 grams) chili powder
- 1 teaspoon (2 grams) dried rosemary
- 1 teaspoon (5 grams) garlic powder
- 1 teaspoon (5 grams) kosher salt
- ½ teaspoon (3 grams) black pepper
- 1 lb. (453 grams) pork tenderloin, membrane removed

Honey Mustard

- ¼ cup (60 grams) Dijon mustard
- 2 tablespoons (30 grams) whole-grain mustard
- 2 tablespoons (30 ml) honey
- 2 teaspoons (10 ml) low-sodium tamari
- 1 garlic clove, grated
- 1 shallot, grated

INSTRUCTIONS

Pork Tenderloin

1. Preheat the air fryer to 380°F (193°C).
2. Mix the brown sugar, smoked paprika, chili powder, dried rosemary, garlic powder, kosher salt, and black pepper in a small bowl.
3. Pat pork tenderloin dry with paper towels, then add the seasoning blend and massage it all over the meat.
4. Bake the pork tenderloin at 380°F (193°C) for 10 minutes.

Honey Mustard

1. Meanwhile, mix the Dijon mustard, whole-grain mustard, honey, tamari, garlic, and shallot in a small bowl until combined. Reserve half of the honey mustard for later.
2. When the pork tenderloin has cooked for 10 minutes, brush the honey mustard on the pork tenderloin. Flip it over and bake it for another 8-15 minutes until it has an internal temperature of 145°F (62°F).
3. Let the pork tenderloin sit for 5 minutes before carving. Serve with the reserved honey mustard sauce.

NUTRITION INFO
SERVING SIZE: 3 OZ. (85 GRAMS) PORK TENDERLOIN

Calories	101 kcal
Carbohydrates	13.5 g
Fats	1.5 g
Protein	6.5 g
Sugar	10.8 g
Sodium	624 mg
Cholesterol	17 mg

Notes

- This recipe is designed for a 4 L basket-style air fryer, 12 L basket-style air fryer, 16 L rack-style air fryer, or 25 L rack-style air fryer.

Tips

1. If the pork tenderloin does not fit into the air fryer basket or rack, cut it in half and air fry it in two batches. Do not try to stuff it into the air fryer, or it will cook unevenly.

SAUSAGE-INFUSED MUSHROOM DELIGHT

Prep Time
10 MINUTES

Cook Time
16 MINUTES

Total Time
26 MINUTES

Serves
3

INGREDIENTS

- ½ lb. (227 grams) mild ground pork sausage
- 8 oz. (226 grams) baby portobello mushrooms
- 4 oz. (113 grams) cream cheese, softened
- 1 shallot
- 1 clove garlic
- ½ teaspoon (3 grams) black pepper
- 2 tablespoons (13 grams) gruyere cheese
- 2 tablespoons (24 grams) roasted red bell peppers, minced
- 1 tablespoon (4 grams) fresh parsley, minced
- 2 tablespoons (11 grams) parmesan cheese
- ¼ cup (30 grams) whole wheat breadcrumbs
- ½ teaspoon (1 gram) Italian seasoning

INSTRUCTIONS

1. Set a medium skillet over medium-high heat. Once the pan gets hot, add the pork sausage and cook for 5-6 minutes, breaking it into small pieces with a wooden spoon until it is browned. Remove it from the heat and set it aside.

2. Preheat the air fryer to 390°F (198°C).

3. Meanwhile, remove the stems from the portobello mushrooms. Set the mushrooms aside and place the stems in a food processor.

4. Add the pork sausage, cream cheese, shallots, garlic, black pepper, gruyere cheese, roasted red bell peppers, and 1 tablespoon (4 grams) of parsley and pulse until finely chopped.

5. Place the remaining parsley, parmesan cheese, breadcrumbs, and Italian seasoning in a small bowl. Mix until combined.

6. Stuff each mushroom with 1 tablespoon (15 grams) of cream cheese sausage filling and place them on a plate.

7. Line the air fryer basket or rack with parchment paper and add the mushrooms.

8. Sprinkle the breadcrumb topping on top of the mushrooms and bake them at 390°F (198°C) for 8-10 minutes.

Notes

- This recipe is designed for a 12 L basket-style air fryer, 16 L rack-style air fryer, or 25 L rack-style air fryer.

- You can cook the mushrooms in a 4 L basket-style air fryer in 3-4 batches.

Tips

1. Note, that if the baby Portobello mushrooms are really small, they may cook in 6-7 minutes.

2. Open the air fryer gently. The mushrooms are small and can easily tip over, which may cause the topping to fall off.

NUTRITION INFO

SERVING SIZE: 4 STUFFED MUSHROOMS	
Calories	296 kcal
Carbohydrates	13.8 g
Fats	20.8 g
Protein	15.7 g
Sugar	0.7 g
Sodium	286 mg
Cholesterol	23 mg

CHAPTER 4
SEAFOOD
RECIPES

DILL AND BASIL SALMON

Prep Time	Cook Time	Total Time	Serves
5 MINUTES	7 MINUTES	12 MINUTES	4

INGREDIENTS

- 4 salmon fillets (about 5 oz. or 142 grams each)
- Juice of ½ lemon
- ¼ teaspoon (1.5 grams) kosher salt
- ¼ teaspoon (1.5 grams) black pepper
- Zest of 1 lemon and juice
- 4 tablespoons (70 grams) plain nonfat Greek yogurt
- 3 fresh basil leaves, minced
- 2 tablespoons (1 gram) fresh dill, minced
- 4 tablespoons (23 grams) grated Parmesan cheese
- Olive oil spray for misting

INSTRUCTIONS

1. Preheat the air fryer to 400°F (204°C).
2. Put the salmon fillets in a large bowl. Add lemon juice, lemon zest, kosher salt, and black pepper, and toss to combine.
3. Mix the Greek yogurt, basil, dill, and 2 tablespoons (11.5 grams) of Parmesan cheese in a small bowl. Mix well until combined.
4. Spread a tablespoon (15 grams) of the yogurt mixture on top of each salmon fillet, then sprinkle the remaining Parmesan cheese.
5. Mist the air fry basket with olive oil spray, then add the salmon fillets to the air fryer and cook them for 7 minutes until fully cooked through.

Notes

- This recipe is designed for a 16 L or 25 L rack-style air fryer.
- You can also cook the salmon fillets in a 4 L or 12 L basket-style air fryer in batches of 2.

Tips

1. If you do not have fresh basil or dill, use 3 teaspoons of dried basil (2.25 grams) and 2 teaspoons (2 grams) of dried dill.
2. Make sure the salmon fillets have the same thickness so they cook evenly.

NUTRITION INFO

SERVING SIZE: 1 SALMON FILLET

Calories	383 kcal
Carbohydrates	4.9 g
Fats	18 g
Protein	50.2 g
Sugar	2.7 g
Sodium	506 mg
Cholesterol	100 mg

SPICY CAJUN SHRIMP AND VEGETABLES

Prep Time
10 MINUTES

Cook Time
10 MINUTES

Total Time
20 MINUTES

Serves
4

INGREDIENTS

- 1 lb. (454 grams) jumbo shrimp, peeled, deveined
- 1 medium zucchini, cut into ¼-inch (6 mm) half-moons
- 1 medium yellow squash, sliced into ¼-inch (6 mm) half-moons
- 2 corn on the cob, cut into ½-inch (1.25 cm) thick pieces
- 1 large red bell pepper, seeded, sliced into ¼-inch (6mm) pieces
- 2 tablespoons (30 ml) avocado oil
- 3 tablespoons (36 grams) Cajun seasoning
- ¼ teaspoon (1.5 grams) kosher salt
- 6 oz. (170 grams) fully cooked turkey Andouille sausage cut into ¼-inch (6 mm) pieces

INSTRUCTIONS

1. Preheat the air fryer to 400°F (204°C).
2. Place shrimp, zucchini, yellow squash, corn, and red bell pepper in a large bowl. Add avocado oil and toss to coat the ingredients in the oil.
3. Add the Cajun seasoning and toss to coat the ingredients in the seasoning.
4. Add the Andouille sausage pieces and toss to combine.
5. Place the ingredients in the air fryer and spread them into an even layer. Cook for 10 minutes at 400°F (204°C) shaking the basket or flipping them over every 3 minutes until the shrimp are fully cooked.

Notes

- This recipe is designed for a 16 L or 25 L rack-style air fryer.
- You can cook the Cajun shrimp and vegetables in a 4 L or 12 L basket-style air fryer in batches of 2.

Tips

1. Cut the vegetables into even-sized pieces so they cook evenly.
2. If you want to reduce the sodium, use salt-free or low-sodium Cajun seasoning.

NUTRITION INFO

SERVING SIZE:
1½ CUPS (448 GRAMS) SHRIMP AND VEGETABLES

Calories	238 kcal
Carbohydrates	15.3 g
Fats	11.9 g
Protein	21.2 g
Sugar	6.8 g
Sodium	544 mg
Cholesterol	61 mg

CRISPY GOLDEN FISH STICKS

Prep Time
10 MINUTES

Cook Time
16 MINUTES

Total Time
26 MINUTES

Serves
4

INGREDIENTS

Tartar Sauce

- ½ cup (125 grams) full-fat Greek yogurt
- ⅓ cup (48 grams) dill pickles, minced
- 1 tablespoon (0.5 grams) fresh dill, minced
- 2 tablespoons (6 grams) fresh chives, minced
- 1 teaspoon (5 grams) fresh lemon juice
- ⅛ teaspoon (0.5 grams) kosher salt
- ⅛ teaspoon (0.5 grams) white pepper
- ½ teaspoon (1.5 grams) garlic powder

Fish Sticks

- 2 large eggs
- 1 tablespoon (15 grams) Dijon mustard
- 1 teaspoon (2 grams) lemon zest
- Juice of ½ lemon
- 1 teaspoon (5 grams) kosher salt
- ½ teaspoon (3 grams) black pepper
- 1 cup (90 grams) whole wheat panko breadcrumbs
- 1 teaspoon (5 grams) Old Bay seasoning
- ½ teaspoon (0.5 grams) dried dill
- 1 1/2 lbs. (448 grams) boneless, skinless wild cod, thawed, cut into 4 x 1 inches (10 cm x 2.5 cm) fish sticks
- Olive oil spray for misting
- 1 lemon, cut into wedges for serving

INSTRUCTIONS

Tartar Sauce

1. Mix Greek yogurt, dill pickles, fresh dill, chives, lemon juice, kosher salt, white pepper, and garlic powder in a small bowl until combined. Cover the sauce with plastic wrap and refrigerate it until you are ready to serve the fish sticks.

Fish Sticks

1. Preheat the air fryer to 400°F (204°C).
2. Whisk eggs in a shallow baking dish until combined. Add Dijon mustard, lemon zest, lemon juice, ½ teaspoon kosher salt (3 grams), and ¼ teaspoon (1.5 grams) black pepper to the eggs and mix until combined.
3. Add the panko breadcrumbs, Old Bay seasoning, dried dill, and the remaining kosher salt and black pepper to another separate shallow baking dish and mix until combined.
4. Dip each fish stick in the egg mixture, then dredge in the panko breadcrumbs. Place the fish on a large plate.
5. Place half of the fish sticks in the air fryer basket in a single layer and mist them lightly with olive oil. Cook for 4 minutes at 400°F (204°C).
6. Flip the fish sticks over and mist them again with olive oil. Cook them for 4 minutes until golden brown.
7. Repeat steps 5-6 to cook the remaining fish sticks.
8. Serve the fish sticks with tartar sauce and lemon wedges.

NUTRITION INFO

SERVING SIZE:
4 FISH STICKS + 2 TABLESPOONS (30 GRAMS) OF TARTAR SAUCE

Calories	116 kcal
Carbohydrates	10.7 g
Fats	2.9 g
Protein	12.1 g
Sugar	6.1 g
Sodium	323 mg
Cholesterol	107 mg

Notes

- This recipe is designed for a 16 L or 25 L rack-style air fryer.
- You can cook the fish sticks in a 4 L basket-style air fryer in 3-4 batches or a 12 L basket-style air fryer in 3 batches.

Tips

1. Gently press the breadcrumbs into each fish stick. This will help prevent the breadcrumbs from flying off the fish as it is cooking in the air fryer.
2. Make sure you cut the fish fillets into even-sized pieces so they cook evenly.

EASY AIR FRYER BACON-WRAPPED SCALLOPS

Prep Time
5 MINUTES

Cook Time
12 MINUTES

Total Time
17 MINUTES

Serves
4

INGREDIENTS

- 16 large sea scallops, cleaned
- 8 slices thick-cut center bacon, cut in half
- 16 metal toothpicks
- ½ teaspoon (1 gram) white pepper
- Avocado oil, for misting
- 2 tablespoons (8 grams) fresh parsley, minced for garnish

NUTRITION INFO

SERVING SIZE: 4 SCALLOPS

Calories	303 kcal
Carbohydrates	0.8 g
Fats	22.2 g
Protein	20.3 g
Sugar	0.7 g
Sodium	557 mg
Cholesterol	58 mg

INSTRUCTIONS

1. Preheat the air fryer to 400°F (204°C).

2. Place the bacon slices in the air fryer basket and cook them for 90 seconds. Turn them over and cook for another 90 seconds. Remove the bacon from the air fryer and place it on a paper towel-lined plate.

3. Pat the scallops dry with paper towels. Wrap a slice of bacon around each scallop and secure it with a toothpick. Repeat until all of the scallops have been wrapped with bacon.

4. Mist both sides of the scallops with avocado oil, then season both sides with white pepper.

5. Place the scallops in the air fryer and cook them for 4 minutes at 400°F (204°C). Flip the scallops over and cook them for another 4 minutes until the bacon is crispy and the scallops are tender.

6. Garnish the bacon-wrapped scallops with parsley.

Notes

- This recipe is designed for a 16 L or 25 L rack-style air fryer.

- You can cook the fish sticks in a 4 L basket-style air fryer in 3-4 batches or a 12 L basket-style air fryer in 2 batches.

Tips

1. Don't skip pre-cooking the bacon. Partially cooking the bacon makes it crispy.

2. Do not cook the bacon pieces too much, or they will break when you wrap them around the scallops. Only cook them for 3 minutes just until the bacon begins to crisp up.

SWEET SMOKY SALMON BITES

Prep Time
5 MINUTES

Cook Time
7 MINUTES

Total Time
12 MINUTES

Serves
4

INGREDIENTS

- 4 skinless salmon fillets (6 oz. or 170 grams each), cut into 1-inch (2.5 cm) cubes
- 2 tablespoons (30 ml) olive oil
- 1 tablespoon (7 grams) smoked paprika
- ¼ teaspoon (0.5 grams) cayenne pepper
- 1 teaspoon (5 grams) garlic powder
- ½ teaspoon (3 grams) dried thyme
- ½ teaspoon (3 grams) dried dill
- 1 teaspoon (5 grams) kosher salt
- ⅛ teaspoon (3 grams) black pepper
- 2 teaspoons (10 grams) brown sugar
- 1 lemon, cut into wedges, for serving
- 2 tablespoons (8 grams) fresh parsley, chopped for garnish

INSTRUCTIONS

1. Preheat the air fryer to 400°F (204°C).

2. Put salmon into a large bowl, add the olive oil, and toss to combine.

3. Mix the smoked paprika, cayenne pepper, garlic powder, dried thyme, dried dill, kosher salt, black pepper, and brown sugar in a small bowl until combined.

4. Sprinkle the seasoning blend over the salmon and toss to coat it in the seasoning.

5. Place the salmon bites in the air fryer and spread them into an even layer. Air fry the salmon bites for 4 minutes at 400°F (204 °C), then shake the basket or turn them over and cook them for another 3 minutes.

6. Place the salmon bites on a serving dish. Garnish the salmon bites with fresh parsley and serve with lemon wedges.

NUTRITION INFO

SERVING SIZE: 1 CUP (159 GRAMS) SALMON BITES	
Calories	306 kcal
Carbohydrates	6.3 g
Fats	15.4 g
Protein	28.1 g
Sugar	1.2 g
Sodium	162 mg
Cholesterol	60 mg

Notes

- This recipe is designed for a 12 L basket-style air fryer, 16 L rack-style air fryer, or 25 L rack-style air fryer.

- You can cook the salmon bites in a 4 L basket-style air fryer in 3-4 batches.

Tips

1. Cut the salmon bites into even-sized pieces so they cook evenly.

2. Let the salmon bites marinate in the fridge for 30 minutes to a few hours for more flavor.

CRISPY FISH SANDWICH

Prep Time
10 MINUTES

Cook Time
10 MINUTES

Total Time
20 MINUTES

Serves
2

INGREDIENTS

Tartar Sauce

- ¼ cup (70 grams) plain full-fat Greek yogurt
- 2 tablespoons (18 grams) dill pickles, minced
- 1 ½ teaspoons (1 gram) fresh dill, minced
- 1 tablespoon (3 grams) fresh chives, minced
- ½ teaspoon (2 ml) fresh lemon juice
- ⅛ teaspoon (0.5 grams) kosher salt
- ⅛ teaspoon (0.5 grams) white pepper
- ¼ teaspoon (1.5 grams) garlic powder

Fish Sandwich

- ½ teaspoon (1.5 grams) garlic powder
- ½ teaspoon (1.5 grams) onion powder
- ½ teaspoon (1.5 grams) black pepper
- 1 teaspoon (5 grams) kosher salt
- 2 cod fillets (5 oz. or 141 grams each)
- 4 tablespoons (30 grams) whole wheat flour
- 1 large egg
- 1 tablespoon (15 ml) fresh lemon juice
- 1/2 tablespoon (9 grams) plain Greek yogurt
- 1/2 cup (60 grams) whole wheat panko breadcrumbs
- Avocado oil, for misting
- 2 whole wheat burger buns
- 2 Romaine lettuce leaves, for serving

INSTRUCTIONS

Tartar Sauce

1. Mix Greek yogurt, dill pickles, fresh dill, chives, lemon juice, kosher salt, white pepper, and garlic powder in a small bowl until combined. Cover the tartar sauce with plastic wrap and refrigerate until you are ready to assemble the fish sandwiches.

Fish Sandwich

1. Preheat the air fryer to 400 °F (204°C).
2. Combine garlic powder and onion powder, black pepper, and kosher salt in a small bowl. Season the cod fillets with the seasoning blend and set them aside.
3. Place whole wheat flour in a shallow baking dish. Whisk egg, lemon juice, and Greek yogurt in a separate shallow baking dish until combined.
4. Place the panko breadcrumbs in another shallow baking dish.
5. Dredge each cod fillet in the flour, then in the egg mixture, and then in the panko breadcrumbs.
6. Place the cod fillets in the air fryer, lightly mist them with avocado oil, and cook for 5 minutes at 400°F (204°C)
7. Flip them over, lightly mist them with olive oil again, and cook them for another 3-5 minutes until golden brown.
8. Toast the whole wheat burger buns if desired, then smear 1 tablespoon (15 grams of tartar sauce) onto each bun and top with a lettuce leaf. Place a cod fillet on each bottom bun, then add the top buns and serve.

NUTRITION INFO

SERVING SIZE: 1 SANDWICH

Calories	335 kcal
Carbohydrates	37.9 g
Fats	6.5 g
Protein	31.3 g
Sugar	8.8 g
Sodium	272 mg
Cholesterol	171 mg

Notes

- This recipe is designed for a 12 L basket-style air fryer, 16 L rack-style air fryer, or 25 L rack-style air fryer.
- You can cook the fish cod fillets in a 4 L basket-style air fryer one at a time.

Tips

1. Leave 1 inch (2.5 cm) of space between each fish fillet. This will help the fish get crispy.
2. Use panko breadcrumbs. You can use regular breadcrumbs to coat the fish fillets, but panko breadcrumbs give the fish fillets a crispy, light coating.

SEAFOOD BLISS SHRIMP TACOS

Prep Time	Cook Time	Total Time	Serves
10 MINUTES	6 MINUTES	16 MINUTES	4

INGREDIENTS

- 1 lb. (454 grams) jumbo shrimp, peeled, deveined
- 2 tablespoons (30 ml) avocado oil
- 1 teaspoon (5 grams) chili powder
- 1 teaspoon (5 grams) garlic powder
- ½ teaspoon (3 grams) ground cumin
- ½ teaspoon (3 grams) onion powder
- ½ teaspoon (3 grams) smoked paprika
- 1 teaspoon (5 grams) kosher salt
- ½ teaspoon (3 grams) black pepper
- 4 6-inch (15 cm) warm flour tortillas
- ¼ cup (22 grams) purple cabbage, finely shredded
- ½ medium avocado, thinly sliced
- ¼ cup (56 grams) Cotija cheese, crumbled
- 4 tablespoons (61 grams) sour cream
- 2 tablespoons (8 grams) fresh cilantro, chopped
- 1 lime, cut into wedges

INSTRUCTIONS

1. Preheat the air fryer to 400°F (204°C).
2. Place shrimp in a large bowl, add avocado oil, and toss to coat.
3. Season shrimp with chili powder, garlic powder, cumin, onion powder, smoked paprika, kosher salt, and black pepper.
4. Place shrimp in the air fryer in a single layer. Cook for 5-6 minutes until cooked through.
5. Place flour tortillas on a taco stand or serving dish. Add 1 tablespoon (15 grams) of cabbage to each tortilla, then top with ½ cup (163 grams) of shrimp, 2 slices of avocado, and a tablespoon (15 grams) of Cotija cheese.
6. Drizzle a tablespoon (25 grams) of sour cream on top of each taco, then garnish with cilantro and serve with lime wedges.

NUTRITION INFO

SERVING SIZE: 1 TACO

Calories	312 kcal
Carbohydrates	18.6 g
Fats	21.4 g
Protein	13 g
Sugar	1.5 g
Sodium	616 mg
Cholesterol	65 mg

Notes

- This recipe is designed for a 12 L basket-style air fryer, 16 L rack-style air fryer, or 25 L rack-style air fryer.
- You can cook the shrimp in a 4 L basket-style air fryer one at a time.

Tips

1. Dry the shrimp with paper towels to ensure the oil and seasonings stick.
2. Marinate the shrimp in the fridge for 30 minutes or up to 3 hours to make the shrimp tacos even tastier.
3. Use Queso fresco if you cannot find Cotija cheese.

THE ULTIMATE CRAB CAKES

Prep Time
5 MINUTES

Cook Time
10 MINUTES

Total Time
15 MINUTES

Serves
4

INGREDIENTS

- 8 oz. (241 grams) lump crab meat
- ¼ medium red bell pepper, minced
- ¼ medium white onion, diced
- 1 clove garlic, grated
- 2 tablespoons (30 grams) mayonnaise
- 3 tablespoons (45 grams) whole wheat crackers, crushed
- 1 tablespoon (15 grams) Dijon mustard
- Zest of ½ lemon
- 1 teaspoon (5 grams) Old Bay seasoning
- Juice of ½ lemon
- Avocado oil, for misting

INSTRUCTIONS

1. Preheat the air fryer to 370°F (187°C).
2. Add lump crab meat, red bell pepper, white onion, garlic, mayonnaise, whole wheat crackers, Dijon mustard, lemon zest, old bay seasoning, and lemon juice, and mix gently until combined.
3. Form the mixture into 4 crab cakes.
4. Place the crab cakes in the air fryer and mist them lightly with avocado oil. Air fry the crab cakes for 10 minutes at 370°F (187°C) until lightly golden and crispy.

Notes

- This recipe is designed for a 12 L basket-style air fryer, 16 L rack-style air fryer, or 25 L rack-style air fryer.
- You can cook the crab cakes in a 4 L basket-style air fryer two at a time.

Tips

1. Make the crab cakes with high-quality lump crab meat for the ultimate flavor and texture.
2. Be gentle with the crab meat. If you mix it too much or break up the meat too much, the crab cakes will have a dense texture.

NUTRITION INFO

SERVING SIZE: 1 CRAB CAKE

Calories	239 kcal
Carbohydrates	10.1 g
Fats	6.2 g
Protein	36.2 g
Sugar	0.7 g
Sodium	427 mg
Cholesterol	161 mg

FLAKY TILAPIA WITH GARLIC AND LEMON PEPPER

Prep Time
10 MINUTES

Cook Time
10 MINUTES

Total Time
20 MINUTES

Serves
2

INGREDIENTS

- 2 tilapia fillets (6 oz. or 22 grams each)
- Olive oil, for misting
- 1½ teaspoon (3 grams) garlic powder
- 1 teaspoon (5 grams) lemon pepper
- ½ teaspoon (3 grams) onion powder
- ½ teaspoon (3 grams) dried dill
- 2 tablespoons (8 grams) fresh parsley for garnish
- 1 lemon, cut into wheels

INSTRUCTIONS

1. Preheat the air fryer to 360°F (182°C).
2. Pat the tilapia fillets dry using paper towels and mist both sides lightly with olive oil.
3. Season both sides of the tilapia with garlic powder, lemon pepper, onion powder, and dried dill.
4. Place the tilapia fillets in the air fryer in a single layer and air fry for 6-10 minutes at 360°F(182°C) until cooked through.

Notes

- This recipe is designed for a 12 L basket-style air fryer, 16 L rack-style air fryer, or 25 L rack-style air fryer.
- You can cook the tilapia in a 4 L basket style air fryer in 2 batches.

Tips

1. If you are afraid the tilapia may stick to the air fryer basket or tray, line it with parchment paper. Note, the bottom of the tilapia may not be as crispy as if it were cooked without parchment paper.
2. If you do not like tilapia, use flounder, rainbow trout, red snapper, or black sea bass fillets instead.

NUTRITION INFO

SERVING SIZE: 1 TILAPIA FILLET

Calories	120 kcal
Carbohydrates	3.1 g
Fats	2.6 g
Protein	22.5 g
Sugar	0.8 g
Sodium	383 mg
Cholesterol	50 mg

LEMON GARLIC BUTTER LOBSTER TAILS

Prep Time	Cook Time	Total Time	Serves
10 MINUTES	10 MINUTES	20 MINUTES	2

INGREDIENTS

Lemon Garlic Butter Sauce

- 2 tablespoons (30 grams) unsalted butter
- 3 cloves of garlic, minced
- 2 tablespoons (8 grams) fresh parsley, minced
- Zest of 1 lemon
- Juice of ½ lemon

Lobster Tails

- 2 (6 oz. or 222 grams) lobster tails, butterflied
- ½ teaspoon (3 grams) paprika
- ½ teaspoon (3 grams) kosher salt
- ½ teaspoon (3 grams) black pepper

INSTRUCTIONS

Lemon Garlic Butter Sauce

1. Place butter in a small skillet, set it over medium-low heat and let it melt.
2. Add the garlic to the melted butter. Cook for 1-2 minutes until fragrant.
3. Stir in the parsley, lemon zest, and lemon juice and mix until combined. Remove it from the heat, reserve half of the sauce for serving, and set it aside.

Lobster Tails

1. Preheat the air fryer to 380°F (193°C).
2. Season lobster tails with paprika, kosher salt, and black pepper.
3. Place them in the air fryer basket, brush them with lemon garlic butter sauce, and cook for 4 minutes at 380°F (193°C).
4. Baste lobster tails with half of the lemon garlic butter sauce and cook them for another 2-4 minutes until cooked through.
5. Serve lobster tails with reserved lemon garlic butter sauce.

Notes

- This recipe is designed for a 4 L basket-style air fryer, 12 L basket-style air fryer, 16 L rack-style air fryer, or 25 L rack-style air fryer.

Tips

1. This recipe has been made using Maine lobsters, but any type of lobster will work. Depending on the size, you may have to cook the lobster tails for more or less time.
2. Use cold water lobster tails for the best results. The meat is more succulent and sweeter.

NUTRITION INFO

SERVING SIZE: 1 LOBSTER TAIL

Calories	214 kcal
Carbohydrates	2.4 g
Fats	12.2 g
Protein	24.6 g
Sugar	0.6 g
Sodium	460 mg
Cholesterol	100 mg

SWEET UMAMI HONEY-GLAZED SALMON

Prep Time	Cook Time	Total Time	Serves
5 MINUTES	10 MINUTES	15 MINUTES	4

INGREDIENTS

- 4 boneless skin-on salmon fillets
- 1 teaspoon (5 grams) kosher salt
- ½ teaspoon (3 grams) black pepper
- 4 tablespoons (60 ml) coconut aminos
- 4 tablespoons (60 ml) honey
- 2 teaspoons (10 grams) sesame seeds

INSTRUCTIONS

1. Preheat the air fryer to 375°F (190°C).
2. Season salmon fillets with kosher salt and black pepper.
3. Brush each salmon fillet with 1 tablespoon (15 ml) of coconut aminos, then place them in the air fryer and cook for 8 minutes at 375°F (190°C) until cooked through.
4. Brush the top of each salmon fillet with 1 tablespoon (15 ml) of honey, then sprinkle ½ teaspoon (1.5 grams) of sesame seeds on top of each.
5. Place the salmon fillets back in the air fryer and cook for 1-2 minutes until the honey starts to caramelize.

Notes

- This recipe is designed for a 12 L basket-style air fryer, 16 L rack-style air fryer, or 25 L rack-style air fryer.
- You can cook the salmon in 2-3 batches in a 4 L basket-style air fryer.

Tips

1. Pat the salmon fillets dry thoroughly with paper towels. This will help the seasonings stick to the fish and give it a beautiful, rich crust.
2. When buying salmon, purchase fillets that are about the same size so they cook evenly.

NUTRITION INFO

SERVING SIZE: 1 SALMON FILLET

Calories	288 kcal
Carbohydrates	20.2 g
Fats	12.3 g
Protein	25.4 g
Sugar	16.2 g
Sodium	89 mg
Cholesterol	0 mg

CRUNCHY TENDER CALAMARI

Prep Time	Cook Time	Total Time	Serves
10 MINUTES	16 MINUTES	26 MINUTES	3

INGREDIENTS

- 8 oz. calamari (227 grams)
- ½ cup (60 grams) whole wheat flour
- 1 large egg
- 2 tablespoons (30 ml) whole milk
- 1 cup (60 grams) whole wheat breadcrumbs
- ½ teaspoon (3 grams) ground paprika
- 1 teaspoon (5 grams) Old Bay seasoning
- ¼ teaspoon (1.5 grams) black pepper
- ⅛ teaspoon (0.5 grams) cayenne pepper
- Avocado oil, for misting

NUTRITION INFO

SERVING SIZE: 1/2 CUP CALAMARI

Calories	274 kcal
Carbohydrates	32.1 g
Fats	8.1 g
Protein	17.1 g
Sugar	0.8 g
Sodium	429 mg
Cholesterol	429 mg

INSTRUCTIONS

1. Preheat the air fryer to 400°F (204°C).

2. Place the whole wheat flour in a shallow baking dish. Whisk egg and milk in a separate shallow baking dish until combined. Place whole wheat breadcrumbs, paprika, Old Bay seasoning, black pepper, and cayenne pepper in a different shallow baking dish and mix until combined.

3. Dredge the calamari in the whole wheat flour, then in the egg mixture, and then in the breadcrumbs making sure to cost them well.

4. Place half the calamari in the air fryer basket or rack and mist lightly with avocado oil. Air fry the calamari for 4 minutes at 400°F (204°C), flip them over, and air fry for another 2-4 minutes until golden and tender. Place the calamari on a serving dish.

5. Repeat step 4 to air fry the remaining calamari.

Notes

- This recipe is designed for a 12 L basket-style air fryer, 16 L rack-style air fryer, or 25 L rack-style air fryer.

- You can cook the calamari in 2-3 batches in a 4 L basket-style air fryer.

Tips

1. Check the calamari often to see if it is done. It can go from tender to tough and rubbery in a few seconds.

2. Let the calamari sit out of the fridge with the coating on for about 5 minutes before air frying them. It will help the coating adhere to the calamari better.

CHAPTER 5
VEGETABLE MAINS AND SIDES RECIPES

CRISPY BROCCOLI

Prep Time
5 MINUTES

Cook Time
10 MINUTES

Total Time
15 MINUTES

Serves
4

INGREDIENTS

- 1 head of broccoli (150 grams), cut into florets
- 2 tablespoons (30 ml) olive oil
- 1 teaspoon (5 grams) garlic powder
- 1 teaspoon (5 grams) onion powder
- 1 teaspoon (5 grams) kosher salt
- 1/2 teaspoon (3 grams) black pepper
- 1/4 teaspoon (1/2 gram) crushed red pepper flakes
- ¼ cup (23 grams) grated Parmesan cheese

INSTRUCTIONS

1. Preheat the air fryer to 370°F (187°C).
2. Place the broccoli in a large bowl.
3. Add olive oil, garlic and onion powder, kosher salt, black pepper, crushed red pepper flakes, and Parmesan cheese to the broccoli. Toss to combine.
4. Place broccoli pieces in the air fryer basket or tray in an even layer. Roast them at 370°F (187°C) for 5 minutes.
5. Shake the basket or turn the broccoli florets over and cook them for another 4-5 minutes until tender.

Notes

- This recipe was designed for a 12 L basket-style air fryer, 16 L rack-style air fryer, or 25 L rack-style air fryer.
- You can cook the broccoli in 2 batches in a 4 L basket-style air fryer.

Tips

1. Use your hands to massage the oil into the broccoli. It will help the tops get crispy.
2. Add a tablespoon of water to the bottom of the basket or tray to prevent the broccoli from burning.

NUTRITION INFO
SERVING SIZE: 1/2 CUP (90 GRAMS) OF BROCCOLI

Calories	92 kcal
Carbohydrates	5.8 g
Fats	7.5 g
Protein	2.7 g
Sugar	1.5 g
Sodium	116 mg
Cholesterol	1 mg

SOY GARLIC BRUSSELS SPROUTS

Prep Time
5 MINUTES

Cook Time
12 MINUTES

Total Time
17 MINUTES

Serves
4

INGREDIENTS

Soy Garlic Sauce

- 3 tablespoons (45 ml) soy sauce
- 2 tablespoons (30 ml) maple syrup
- 1 teaspoon (5 ml) toasted sesame oil
- 1 teaspoon (5 ml) rice wine vinegar
- 1/2 teaspoon (2.5 grams) spicy Thai chili paste
- 1 teaspoon (2 grams) grated ginger
- 2 garlic cloves, minced
- 1 teaspoon (3 grams) sesame seeds

Brussels Sprouts

- 1 lb. (453 grams) Brussels sprouts, washed, stems removed, halved
- 2 tablespoons (30 ml) olive oil
- 1 teaspoon (5 grams) garlic powder
- 1 teaspoon (5 grams) onion powder
- ½ teaspoon (3 grams) black pepper
- ¼ teaspoon (1.5 grams) kosher salt

INSTRUCTIONS

Soy Garlic Sauce

1. Whisk the soy sauce, maple syrup, toasted sesame oil, rice wine vinegar, chili paste, ginger, garlic, and sesame seeds in a small bowl until combined. Set it aside.

Brussels Sprouts

1. Preheat the air fryer to 380°F (193°C).
2. Place the Brussels sprouts in a large bowl. Add olive oil, garlic and onion powder, black pepper, and kosher salt. Toss until the sprouts are coated in the oil and seasonings.
3. Arrange the sprouts in the air fryer basket in a single layer. Roast for 6 minutes at 380°F (193°C).
4. Shake the basket or flip the Brussels sprouts over and cook them for another 6 minutes until tender.
5. Place the cooked sprouts in a large bowl, then pour the soy garlic sauce over it and toss until combined.

NUTRITION INFO
SERVING SIZE: 1/2 CUP (90 GRAMS) OF BRUSSELS SPROUTS

Calories	147 kcal
Carbohydrates	8.1 g
Fats	10.6 g
Protein	0.6 g
Sugar	5.5 g
Sodium	709 mg
Cholesterol	0 mg

Notes

- This recipe was designed for a 12 L basket-style air fryer, 16 L rack-style air fryer, or 25 L rack-style air fryer.
- You can cook the Brussels sprouts in 2 batches in a 4 L basket-style air fryer.

Tips

1. Pat the Brussels sprouts dry after you wash them to get rid of the excess moisture. It will help the olive oil and seasonings stick to them.
2. Buy Brussels sprouts that are roughly the same size so they cook evenly.

PARMESAN AND HERB SWEET POTATOES

Prep Time
10 MINUTES

Cook Time
15 MINUTES

Total Time
25 MINUTES

Serves
4

INGREDIENTS

- 1 teaspoon (3 grams) herbs de Provence
- 1 teaspoon (1.20 grams) dried rosemary
- 1 teaspoon (5 grams) garlic powder
- 1/2 teaspoon (3 grams) onion powder
- 1/2 teaspoon (3 grams) kosher salt
- 1/4 teaspoon (1.5 grams) black pepper
- 3/4 cup (67 grams) grated Parmesan cheese
- 2 medium sweet potatoes, cut into ⅛-inch (3 mm) thick slices
- 2 tablespoons (15 ml) olive oil

INSTRUCTIONS

1. Preheat the air fryer to 400°F (204°C).

2. Mix the herbs de Provence, rosemary, garlic powder, onion powder, kosher salt, black pepper, and Parmesan cheese in a small bowl until combined.

3. Place sweet potatoes in a large bowl. Add olive oil, and toss to coat them in the oil.

4. Add the Parmesan cheese mixture to the sweet potatoes. Toss to coat them in the cheese.

5. Place the sweet potato slices in an air fryer pan in an even layer and cook for 15 minutes at 400°F (204°C) until they are tender in the center and crispy around the edges.

Notes

- This recipe was designed for a 16 L rack-style air fryer or 25 L rack-style air fryer.
- You can cook the Parmesan herb sweet potatoes in 2 batches in a 4 L or 12 L basket-style air fryer.

Tips

1. Cut the sweet potatoes into uniform slices so they cook evenly.

2. Use a mandoline to cut the sweet potatoes into ⅛-inch (3 mm) thick slices.

NUTRITION INFO

SERVING SIZE: 1/2 CUP (75 GRAMS) OF SWEET POTATOES

Calories	129 kcal
Carbohydrates	16.6 g
Fats	7.3 g
Protein	1.4 g
Sugar	3.5 g
Sodium	81 mg
Cholesterol	1 mg

SPICY CAULIFLOWER

Prep Time	Cook Time	Total Time	Serves
5 MINUTES	15 MINUTES	20 MINUTES	4

INGREDIENTS

- 1 medium head of cauliflower, cut into florets
- 1 tablespoon (15 ml) olive oil
- 1 teaspoon (5 grams) kosher salt
- ½ teaspoon (3 grams) black pepper
- ¼ teaspoon (1.5 grams) curry powder
- ½ teaspoon (1 gram) ground thyme
- ½ teaspoon (3 grams) smoked paprika
- 1 teaspoon (5 grams) garlic powder

INSTRUCTIONS

1. Preheat the air fryer to 390°F (198°C).

2. Put cauliflower florets in a large bowl. Add olive oil, kosher salt, black pepper, curry powder, thyme, smoked paprika, and garlic powder. Toss to combine.

3. Place the cauliflower florets into the air fryer in a single layer and roast them at 390°F (198°C) for 15 minutes, shaking the basket or flipping them over every 3 minutes until they are tender.

Notes

- This recipe was designed for a 12 L basket-style air fryer, 16 L rack-style air fryer, or 25 L rack-style air fryer.
- You can cook the cauliflower in 2 batches in a 4 L basket-style air fryer.

Tips

1. Cut the cauliflower into uniform pieces so they cook evenly.
2. Place a tablespoon (15 grams) of water in the bottom of the air fryer to prevent the cauliflower from burning.

NUTRITION INFO

SERVING SIZE: 1/2 CUP (90 GRAMS) OF CAULIFLOWER

Calories	37 kcal
Carbohydrates	1.4 g
Fats	3.5 g
Protein	0.5 g
Sugar	0.5 g
Sodium	80 mg
Cholesterol	0 mg

DELIGHTFULLY CRISPY FRENCH FRIES

Prep Time
10 MINUTES

Cook Time
10 MINUTES

Total Time
20 MINUTES

Serves
4

INGREDIENTS

- 4 large russet potatoes washed, peeled, and cut into ¼-inch (6 mm) fries
- 2 tablespoons (30 ml) olive oil
- 1 teaspoon (5 grams) sea salt
- 1 teaspoon (5 grams) garlic powder
- ½ teaspoon (3 grams) paprika
- ½ teaspoon (3 grams) black pepper

INSTRUCTIONS

1. Preheat the air fryer to 375°F (190°C).
2. Place the fries in a large bowl and add olive oil. Toss to coat them in the oil.
3. Add sea salt, garlic powder, paprika, and black pepper and toss to coat the fries in the seasoning.
4. Put the fries in the air fryer basket or rack in a single layer. Air fry at 375°F (190°C) for 10-15 minutes until golden brown and crispy.

Notes

- This recipe is designed for a 12 L basket-style air fryer, 16 L rack-style air fryer, or 25 L rack-style air fryer.
- You can cook the fries in a 4 L basket-style air fryer in 2-3 batches.

Tips

1. Cut the fries into even-sized pieces so they cook evenly.
2. Do not overcrowd the basket or rack, or the fries will be soggy instead of crispy.

NUTRITION INFO

SERVING SIZE: ½ CUP OF FRIES (80 GRAMS)

Calories	160 kcal
Carbohydrates	26 g
Fats	7 g
Protein	4 g
Sugar	3 g
Sodium	117 mg
Cholesterol	0 mg

CHILI SWEET POTATO FRIES

Prep Time
5 MINUTES

Cook Time
12 MINUTES

Total Time
17 MINUTES

Serves
2

INGREDIENTS

- 2 medium sweet potatoes, peeled, cut into 1/4-inch (6 mm) fries
- 2 teaspoons (10 ml) avocado oil
- 2 teaspoons (6 grams) chili powder
- ½ teaspoon (3 grams) sea salt
- ¼ teaspoon (1.5 grams) garlic powder
- ¼ teaspoon (1.5 grams) onion powder
- ½ teaspoon (3 grams) smoked paprika
- ¼ teaspoon (1.5 grams) black pepper

INSTRUCTIONS

1. Preheat the air fryer to 380°F (193°C).

2. Put sweet potato fries in a large bowl and add avocado oil. Toss to coat the sweet potato fries in the oil.

3. Add chili powder, sea salt, garlic powder, onion powder, smoked paprika, and black pepper. Toss to coat the fries in the seasoning.

4. Arrange sweet potato fries in the air fryer basket or tray in a single layer. Air fry at 380°F (193°C) for 6 minutes.

5. Shake the basket or turn the fries over and cook for another 6 minutes until golden brown and crispy.

Notes

- This recipe is designed for a 12 L basket-style air fryer, 16 L rack-style air fryer, or 25 L rack-style air fryer.
- You can cook sweet potato fries in a 4 L basket-style air fryer in 2-3 batches.

Tips

1. Use sweet potatoes that are roughly the same size and cut them into uniform fries so they cook evenly.

2. Season the fries with 1/4 teaspoon (1.5 grams) of kosher salt right after you take them out of the air fryer for even more flavor.

NUTRITION INFO

SERVING SIZE: ½ CUP OF SWEET POTATO FRIES (80 GRAMS)

Calories	251 kcal
Carbohydrates	33.2 g
Fats	13.8 g
Protein	2 g
Sugar	7 g
Sodium	162 mg
Cholesterol	0 mg

ZESTY GREEN BEANS

Prep Time
5 MINUTES

Cook Time
10 MINUTES

Total Time
15 MINUTES

Serves
4

INGREDIENTS

- 1 lb. (454 grams) fresh green beans, trimmed
- 1 tablespoon (15 ml) olive oil
- 3/4 teaspoon (4 grams) kosher salt
- ½ teaspoon (3 grams) garlic powder
- ¼ teaspoon (1.5 grams) onion powder
- ¼ teaspoon (1.5 grams) black pepper
- 1/2 lemon

INSTRUCTIONS

1. Preheat the air fryer to 380°F (193°C).

2. Place the green beans in a large bowl and add the olive oil, kosher salt, garlic powder, onion powder, and black pepper. Toss to combine.

3. Put green beans in the air fryer basket or tray in a single layer. Air fry at 380°F (193°C) for 5 minutes.

4. Shake the basket or flip the green beans over and cook them for another 4-5 minutes until tender.

5. Squeeze the lemon over the green beans before serving.

Notes

- This recipe is designed for a 12 L basket-style air fryer, 16 L rack-style air fryer, or 25 L rack-style air fryer.
- Cook the green beans in a 4 L basket-style air fryer in 2 batches.

Tips

1. Cut large green beans in half to make them the same size. This will help them cook evenly.

2. The green beans will become soft after a while, so serve them immediately after you take them out of the air fryer.

NUTRITION INFO

SERVING SIZE: ½ CUP OF GREEN BEANS (60 GRAMS)

Calories	38 kcal
Carbohydrates	2.2 g
Fats	3.5 g
Protein	0.4 g
Sugar	0.8 g
Sodium	134 mg
Cholesterol	0 mg

SWEET AND BUTTERY CORN ON THE COB

Prep Time
5 MINUTES

Cook Time
8 MINUTES

Total Time
13 MINUTES

Serves
2

INGREDIENTS

- 2 ears of sweet corn, husk and silk removed, cut in half horizontally
- 1 tablespoon (15 ml) avocado oil
- 1/2 teaspoon (3 grams) sea salt
- 1/2 teaspoon (3 grams) black pepper
- 3 tablespoons (15 ml) butter, melted
- 2 tablespoons (8 grams) fresh parsley, chopped

INSTRUCTIONS

1. Preheat the air fryer to 380°F (193°C).
2. Brush each piece of corn all over with olive oil, then put them in the air fryer basket or tray.
3. Air fry at 380°F (193°C) for 4 minutes, then turn the corn over and cook them for another 4 minutes.
4. Brush each side of the corn on the cob with melted butter, then sprinkle with sea salt and black pepper. Garnish with fresh parsley.

Notes

- This recipe is designed for a 12 L basket-style air fryer, 16 L rack-style air fryer, or 25 L rack-style air fryer.
- You can cook the corn in a 4 L basket-style air fryer for 2 at a time.

Tips

1. Buy the freshest corn possible. Each ear of corn should have brown but tacky silk and a bright green husk with few to no brown spots. The corn should feel firm when you squeeze it with your hand.
2. You do not have to cut the corn on the cob in half. However, it will take longer to cook if you don't. Cook the corn for 10-15 minutes at 380°F (193°C).

NUTRITION INFO

SERVING SIZE: 2 PIECES OF CORN

Calories	291 kcal
Carbohydrates	18 g
Fats	24.4 g
Protein	3.1 g
Sugar	5 g
Sodium	277 mg
Cholesterol	45 mg

SAVORY HERBED CARROTS

Prep Time
10 MINUTES

Cook Time
20 MINUTES

Total Time
30 MINUTES

Serves
4

INGREDIENTS

- 1 lb. (453 grams) medium carrots, washed, peeled
- 2 tablespoons (30 ml) olive oil
- 1 teaspoon (3 grams) fresh thyme
- 1 teaspoon (5 grams) kosher salt
- 1/2 teaspoon (3 grams) black pepper
- ½ teaspoon (3 grams) garlic powder
- 1/4 teaspoon (1.5 grams) onion powder
- ½ teaspoon (3 grams) paprika
- 1/4 cup (22 grams) grated Parmesan cheese
- 2 tablespoons (8 grams) fresh parsley, chopped

INSTRUCTIONS

1. Preheat the air fryer to 380°F (193°C).
2. Place the carrots in a large bowl.
3. Add olive oil, thyme, kosher salt, black pepper, garlic powder, onion powder, and paprika. Toss to combine.
4. Place the carrots in the air fryer in an even layer and air fry at 380°F (193°C) for 10 minutes.
5. Shake the basket or flip the carrots over and cook them for another 8-10 minutes until tender.
6. Place the carrots on a serving platter and top with Parmesan cheese and fresh parsley.

Notes

- This recipe is designed for a 12 L basket-style air fryer, 16 L rack-style air fryer, or 25 L rack-style air fryer.
- You can cook the carrots in a 4 L basket-style air fryer in 2 batches.

Tips

1. You can use baby carrots instead of larger carrots. Just cut the cooking time down to 8-9 minutes and flip or shake the basket halfway through.
2. Dry the carrots thoroughly with paper towels after washing them. The carrots will develop a mushy texture if you air fry them while they are wet.

NUTRITION INFO

SERVING SIZE: ½ CUP OF CARROTS (75 GRAMS)

Calories	72 kcal
Carbohydrates	2.6 g
Fats	7.1 g
Protein	0.4 g
Sugar	1.3 g
Sodium	98 mg
Cholesterol	0 mg

CRISPY AVOCADO TACOS

Prep Time
15 MINUTES

Cook Time
8 MINUTES

Total Time
23 MINUTES

Serves
4 TACOS

INGREDIENTS

- 2 medium avocados
- 1/2 teaspoon (1 gram) chili powder
- 1/2 teaspoon (3 grams) garlic powder
- 1/2 teaspoon (3 grams) onion powder
- 1/2 teaspoon (3 grams) kosher salt
- 1/2 teaspoon (3 grams) black pepper
- 1/4 teaspoon (0.25 grams) dried oregano
- 1 cup (60 grams) whole wheat panko breadcrumbs
- 4 corn 6-inch (15 cm) tortillas
- 1 Roma tomato, diced
- 1/4 cup (22 grams) red cabbage, finely shredded
- 1/4 cup (60 grams) vegan sour cream
- 2 tablespoons (8 grams) fresh cilantro, chopped
- 1 lime, cut into wedges

INSTRUCTIONS

1. Preheat the air fryer to 370°F (190°C).

2. Cut each avocado in half, then cut each half into 3 pieces and place them in a large bowl.

3. Combine chili powder, garlic powder, onion powder, kosher salt, black pepper, and oregano in a small bowl. Sprinkle the half of the seasoning blend over the avocados and toss gently to combine.

4. Place breadcrumbs in a shallow baking dish, add the remaining seasoning blend and mix to combine.

5. Press both sides of each avocado into the breadcrumbs, then place them on a plate.

6. Add half of the avocado slices to the air fryer basket or tray in an even layer and air fry at 370°F (190°C) for 4 minutes.

7. Remove the avocado slices from the air fryer, place them on a plate, and repeat step 6 to cook the remaining half of the avocados.

8. To assemble the tacos, place the corn tortillas on a serving platter.

9. Add 3 avocado slices to each tortilla, then top with tomatoes, red cabbage, sour cream, and cilantro and serve with lime wedges.

NUTRITION INFO

SERVING SIZE: 1 TACO

Calories	253 kcal
Carbohydrates	28.8 g
Fats	15.2 g
Protein	4.6 g
Sugar	3.2 g
Sodium	89 mg
Cholesterol	0 mg

Notes

- This recipe is designed for a 12 L basket-style air fryer, 16 L rack-style air fryer, or 25 L rack-style air fryer.

- You can cook the avocado slices in a 4 L basket-style air fryer in 3 batches.

Tips

1. Use firm but ripe avocados. If the avocados are too soft, they will be difficult to handle.

2. Do not slice the avocados too thinly, or they may break apart as you are breading them.

HERB-ROASTED VEGETABLE MEDLEY

Prep Time
10 MINUTES

Cook Time
15 MINUTES

Total Time
25 MINUTES

Serves
4

INGREDIENTS

- 1 medium red bell pepper, cut into 1/2-inch (1.25 cm) pieces
- 1 medium red onion, cut into 1/2-inch (1.25 cm) pieces
- 1 medium zucchini, sliced into 1/2-inch (1.25 cm) pieces
- 1 medium yellow squash, sliced into 1/2-inch (1.25 cm) pieces
- 1 small eggplant, cut into 1/2-inch (1.25 cm) pieces
- 1 tablespoon (15 ml) olive oil
- 1 teaspoon (5 grams) garlic powder
- 2 teaspoons (2 grams) fresh thyme
- 1 teaspoon (1 gram)fresh rosemary
- 1 teaspoon (5 grams) kosher salt
- ½ teaspoon (3 grams) black pepper
- 1/2 teaspoon (2 grams) crushed red pepper flakes

INSTRUCTIONS

1. Preheat the air fryer to 375°F (190°C).
2. Place the red bell pepper, onion, zucchini, squash, and eggplant in a large bowl.
3. Add olive oil and toss to combine. Add garlic powder, thyme, rosemary, kosher salt, black pepper, and crushed red pepper flakes. Toss to combine.
4. Place the vegetables in a single layer in the air fryer. Cook at 375°F (190°C) for 7 minutes.
5. Shake the basket or flip the vegetables over and cook for another 5-8 minutes until tender.

NUTRITION INFO
SERVING SIZE: 1 CUP (75 GRAMS) OF VEGETABLES

Calories	90 kcal
Carbohydrates	12 g
Fats	3.9 g
Protein	2.9 g
Sugar	6.6 g
Sodium	97 mg
Cholesterol	0 mg

Notes

- This recipe is designed for a 12 L basket-style air fryer, 16 L rack-style air fryer, or 25 L rack-style air fryer.
- You can cook the vegetables in a 4 L basket-style air fryer in 2 batches.

Tips

1. Cut vegetables into pieces that are roughly the same size. It will help them cook evenly and ensure they finish cooking around the same time.
2. Do not overcrowd the basket or tray. Arrange the vegetables in a single layer so they do not steam, and to cook evenly.

FOUR INGREDIENT VEGGIE PASTA BAKE

Prep Time
10 MINUTES

Cook Time
10 MINUTES

Total Time
20 MINUTES

Serves
4

INGREDIENTS

- 8 oz. (250 grams) whole wheat penne pasta
- 2 cups (300 grams) frozen stir fry vegetables, thawed, chopped
- 2 1/4 cups (500 gram) marinara sauce
- 1 cup (120 grams) shredded cheddar cheese

INSTRUCTIONS

1. Cook penne pasta in salted boiling water using the manufacturer's directions. Drain it and place it in a large bowl.

2. Preheat the air fryer to 360°F (182°C).

3. Add the stir-fried vegetables and marinara sauce to the pasta and mix until combined. Transfer it to an air fryer cake pan and sprinkle cheddar cheese on top of the pasta bake.

4. Air fry pasta bake for 10 minutes at 360°F (182°C) until the cheese melts and is golden brown.

NUTRITION INFO

SERVING SIZE: 1 CUP
(200 GRAMS) OF PASTA BAKE

Calories	90 kcal
Carbohydrates	12 g
Fats	3.9 g
Protein	2.9 g
Sugar	6.6 g
Sodium	97 mg
Cholesterol	0 mg

Notes

- This recipe is designed for a 12 L basket-style air fryer, 16 L rack-style air fryer, or 25 L rack-style air fryer.

- If you are using a 4 L basket-style air fryer, divide the pasta bake between 2 x 6-inch (15 cm) cake pans, top with cheddar cheese, and air fry them individually.

Tips

1. Cook penne pasta until it is al dente. It will develop a mushy texture if it is overcooked.

2. Use frozen mixed vegetables if you cannot find frozen stir-fry vegetables.

3. If you do not have an air fryer cake pan, use an oven-safe baking dish that can fit in your air fryer.

CHAPTER 6
BREAD AND SNACK RECIPES

PARMESAN GARLIC BREAD

Prep Time	Cook Time	Total Time	Serves
10 MINUTES	10 MINUTES	20 MINUTES	8

INGREDIENTS

- 1/2 cup (115 grams) butter, softened
- 5 cloves garlic, minced
- 2 tablespoons (8 grams) fresh parsley
- 1/2 teaspoon (3 grams) kosher salt
- 1/4 teaspoon (1.5 grams) white pepper
- 1/4 cup (22 grams) grated Parmesan cheese
- 1/2 whole wheat French bread, cut into 8 x 1-inch (2.5 cm) thick slices

INSTRUCTIONS

1. Preheat the air fryer to 350°F (176°C).

2. Place butter, garlic, parsley, kosher salt, white pepper, and Parmesan cheese in a small bowl. Mix until combined.

3. Spread 1 tablespoon (15 grams) of the garlic butter on each French bread slice.

4. Place half of the garlic bread in the air fryer, buttered side up. Air fry the garlic bread at 350°F (176°C) for 5 minutes until golden brown.

5. Repeat step 4 until all of the garlic bread has been air-fried.

NUTRITION INFO

**SERVING SIZE:
1 GARLIC BREAD SLICE**

Calories	89 kcal
Carbohydrates	2.1 g
Fats	8.6 g
Protein	0.8 g
Sugar	0.2 g
Sodium	118 mg
Cholesterol	20 mg

Notes

- This recipe is designed for a 12 L basket-style air fryer, 16 L rack-style air fryer, or 25 L rack-style air fryer.

- If you are using a 4 L basket-style air fryer, cook the garlic bread in 3-4 batches.

Tips

1. Line the air fryer basket or tray with foil or parchment paper. It will keep the bottom of the garlic bread from becoming overly crispy.

2. Do not stack the garlic bread slices on top of one another or the bread will be soggy.

SMOKY BBQ POTATO CHIPS

Prep Time
5 MINUTES

Cook Time
25 MINUTES

Total Time
30 MINUTES

Serves
2

INGREDIENTS

- 2 medium Yukon gold potatoes
- 2 tablespoons (30 ml) olive oil
- 1 ½ teaspoons (7 grams) kosher salt
- 1 ½ teaspoons (7 grams) smoked paprika
- ½ teaspoon (2 grams) cayenne pepper
- 1 ½ teaspoons (7 grams) garlic powder
- 1 teaspoon (6 grams) onion powder
- 1 teaspoon (4 grams) granulated sugar

INSTRUCTIONS

1. Preheat the air fryer to 200°F (93°C).
2. Use a mandoline or a sharp knife to cut each potato into very thin 1/16-inch (1.5 mm) slices. Place them in a large bowl.
3. Add olive oil, kosher salt, smoked paprika, cayenne pepper, garlic powder, onion powder, and sugar. Toss to coat potatoes in the oil and seasonings.
4. Place the potato chips in a single layer on the air fryer trays. Air fry potato chips for 20 minutes at 200°F (93°C).
5. Flip the potato chips over, increase the temperature to 400°F (204°C), and cook the potato chips for another 5 minutes until golden brown.

Notes

- This recipe is designed for a 16 L rack-style air fryer or 25 L rack-style air fryer.
- If you are using a 4 L basket-style air fryer or 12 L basket-style air fryer, cook the potato chips in 3-4 batches.

Tips

1. Rinse the potato slices with cold water to remove some of the starch before air frying them. This will help make the chips super crunchy.
2. Pat the potatoes properly and dry them with paper towels. The drier they are, the crispier they will be once they are cooked.

NUTRITION INFO

SERVING SIZE: 1/2 CUP (10 GRAMS) POTATO CHIPS

Calories	99 kcal
Carbohydrates	16.5 g
Fats	3.5 g
Protein	1.3 g
Sugar	1.8 g
Sodium	72 mg
Cholesterol	0 mg

RANCH KALE CHIPS

Prep Time
5 MINUTES

Cook Time
5 MINUTES

Total Time
10 MINUTES

Serves
4

INGREDIENTS

- 1 bunch (2 cups or 137 grams) of kale, washed, dried, stems removed
- 1 tablespoon (15 ml) olive oil
- ¼ teaspoon (1.5 grams) kosher salt
- ½ teaspoon (0.5 grams) dried dill
- ½ teaspoon (0.5 grams) dried chives
- ½ teaspoon (1.5 grams) garlic powder
- ½ teaspoon (1.5 grams) onion powder

INSTRUCTIONS

1. Preheat the air fryer to 375°F (190°C).
2. Tear the kale into bite-sized pieces and place them in a large bowl.
3. Add the olive oil and massage it into the kale leaves with your hands.
4. Place the kosher salt, dried dill, chives, garlic, and onion powder in a small bowl. Mix until combined.
5. Sprinkle the ranch seasoning on top of the kale chips and toss to coat them in the seasonings.
6. Put kale chips in the air fryer basket or tray in an even layer and air fry at 375°F (190°C) for 4-5 minutes.

Notes

- This recipe is designed for a 12 L basket-style air fryer, 16 L rack-style air fryer, or 25 L rack-style air fryer.
- If you are using a 4 L basket-style air fryer, cook the kale chips in 2 batches.

Tips

1. Make sure each piece of kale gets a thin coating of oil when you are massaging the oil into it. It will help the seasonings stick and help the chips develop a crispy texture.
2. Uncurl the kale leaves when you are placing them in the air fryer basket or tray to ensure they become crispy all over.

NUTRITION INFO

SERVING SIZE: 1/2 CUP (18 GRAMS) KALE CHIPS

Calories	75 kcal
Carbohydrates	3.8 g
Fats	3.8 g
Protein	3 g
Sugar	3 g
Sodium	84 mg
Cholesterol	1 mg

CAJUN PORTOBELLO MUSHROOM FRIES

Prep Time	**Cook Time**	**Total Time**	**Serves**
10 MINUTES	7 MINUTES	17 MINUTES	2

INGREDIENTS

- ⅓ cup (40 grams) whole wheat flour
- 2 large eggs
- 1 cup (60 grams) whole wheat panko breadcrumbs
- 1 teaspoon (2 grams) Italian seasoning
- 1 ¼ teaspoons (6 grams) Cajun seasoning
- 2 (about 3 oz. or 85 grams each) portobello mushrooms, cleaned, stems and gills removed, cut into 1-inch (2.5 cm) strips
- Olive oil spray for misting

INSTRUCTIONS

1. Preheat the air fryer to 390°F (198°C).
2. Mix the whole wheat flour and 1/4 teaspoon (1 gram) of Cajun seasoning in a shallow baking dish until combined. Place the eggs in another shallow baking dish and whisk until combined.
3. Place the breadcrumbs, Italian seasoning, and the remaining Cajun seasoning in a third separate shallow baking dish and mix until combined.
4. Dredge each portobello mushroom strip in the flour, then in the eggs, and then in the bread crumbs. Place them in the air fryer basket or tray.
5. Mist the portobello mushroom fries lightly with olive oil and air fry at 390°F (198°C) for 4 minutes.
6. Flip the portobello mushroom fries over and air fry them for another 3 minutes until crispy.

Notes

- This recipe is designed for a 12 L basket-style air fryer, 16 L rack-style air fryer, or 25 L rack-style air fryer.
- If you are using a 4 L basket-style air fryer, cook the potato chips in 2 batches.

Tips

1. Cut the portobello mushrooms into even-sized pieces.
2. Clean the portobello mushrooms using a damp paper towel. Do not soak them in water. They will soak up the water, making it difficult to air fry them crisply.

NUTRITION INFO

SERVING SIZE: 1 CUP (134 GRAMS) OF PORTOBELLO MUSHROOM FRIES

Calories	148 kcal
Carbohydrates	14.7 g
Fats	5.4 g
Protein	11.6 g
Sugar	0.9 g
Sodium	90 mg
Cholesterol	186 mg

BUFFALO CAULIFLOWER

Prep Time	Cook Time	Total Time	Serves
5 MINUTES	**15 MINUTES**	**20 MINUTES**	**4**

INGREDIENTS

- 1 medium head of cauliflower, cut into bite-sized florets
- 1 cup (240 ml) buffalo sauce
- 2 tablespoons (30 ml) olive oil
- 1 teaspoon (5 grams) garlic powder
- 1/2 teaspoon (3 grams) onion powder
- ½ teaspoon (3 grams) kosher salt
- Olive oil, for misting
- 1/2 cup of (120 grams) Ranch dressing

INSTRUCTIONS

1. Preheat the air fryer to 375°F (190°C).
2. Place cauliflower florets in a large bowl. Add buffalo sauce, olive oil, garlic powder, onion powder, and kosher salt. Toss to combine.
3. Mist the air fryer basket or tray with olive oil. Place the buffalo cauliflower in the air fryer in a single layer and air fry for 12-15 minutes at 375°F (190°C) until tender.
4. Serve the buffalo cauliflower with ranch dressing.

Notes

- This recipe is designed for a 12 L basket-style air fryer, 16 L rack-style air fryer, or 25 L rack-style air fryer.
- If you are using a 4 L basket-style air fryer, cook the buffalo cauliflower in 2 batches.

Tips

1. Use blue cheese dressing as a substitute for ranch dressing.
2. Let the excess buffalo sauce drip off the cauliflower before placing it in the air fryer basket or tray. Excess sauce can cause the cauliflower to develop a mushy texture.

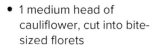

NUTRITION INFO
SERVING SIZE: 1 CUP (325 GRAMS) OF BUFFALO CAULIFLOWER

Calories	192 kcal
Carbohydrates	3 g
Fats	19.8 g
Protein	0.7 g
Sugar	1 g
Sodium	614 mg
Cholesterol	3 mg

PARMESAN AVOCADO FRIES

Prep Time
5 MINUTES

Cook Time
7 MINUTES

Total Time
12 MINUTES

Serves
4

INGREDIENTS

- 4 medium-sized, slightly under-ripe avocados, peeled
- 1/3 cup (40 grams) whole wheat flour
- 1/4 teaspoon (1.5 grams) smoked paprika
- 1/2 teaspoon (3 grams) garlic powder
- 1/4 teaspoon (1.5 grams) onion powder
- 1/4 teaspoon (1.5 grams) kosher salt
- 1 large egg
- 1/2 cup (60 grams) whole wheat panko breadcrumbs
- 1/2 cup (45 grams) grated Parmesan cheese
- Avocado oil, for misting

INSTRUCTIONS

1. Preheat the air fryer to 390°F (198°C).
2. Cut each avocado in half, then cut each half into 3 pieces and place them in a large bowl.
3. Place the whole wheat flour, smoked paprika, garlic and onion powder, and kosher salt in a shallow baking dish and mix until combined.
4. Whisk the egg in a separate shallow baking dish until combined.
5. Mix breadcrumbs and Parmesan cheese in another shallow baking dish until combined.
6. Dredge each avocado piece in the flour, then in the eggs, then in the breadcrumbs, and place them on a plate.
7. Mist the air fryer basket or tray with avocado oil, then place the avocado fries in the air fryer in a single layer.
8. Air fry the avocado fries for 4 minutes at 390°F (198°C), then flip them over and cook them for another 3 minutes.

Notes

- This recipe is designed for a 12 L basket-style air fryer, 16 L rack-style air fryer, or 25 L rack-style air fryer.
- If you are using a 4 L basket-style air fryer, cook the avocado fries in 2 batches.

Tips

1. Use slightly under-ripe avocados. They won't break while you are breading them.
2. Gently press the avocado fries into the breadcrumb mixture to ensure they are evenly coated.

NUTRITION INFO

**SERVING SIZE: 1/2 CUP
(6 AVOCADO FRIES OR 120 GRAMS)
OF AVOCADO FRIES**

Calories	192 kcal
Carbohydrates	3 g
Fats	19.8 g
Protein	0.7 g
Sugar	1 g
Sodium	614 mg
Cholesterol	3 mg

CHEESY CRISPY RAVIOLI WITH WARM MARINARA SAUCE

Prep Time
5 MINUTES

Cook Time
7 MINUTES

Total Time
12 MINUTES

Serves
4

INGREDIENTS

- 2 large eggs
- 2 cups (180 grams) whole wheat panko bread crumbs
- 1/2 cup (45 grams) Parmesan cheese, grated
- 1/4 teaspoon (1.5 grams) sea salt
- 2 teaspoons (10 grams) garlic powder
- 1 teaspoon (2 grams) Italian seasoning
- 1 teaspoon (5 grams) onion powder
- 1 12 oz. (340 grams) bag of frozen mini cheese ravioli, thawed
- Olive oil, for misting
- 1 cup (264 grams) warm marinara sauce for serving

INSTRUCTIONS

1. Preheat the air fryer to 400°F (204°C).

2. Whisk eggs in a small bowl until combined.

3. Place the bread crumbs, Parmesan cheese, sea salt, garlic powder, Italian seasoning, and onion powder in a shallow baking dish. Mix until combined.

4. Dredge the ravioli in the eggs, then in the breadcrumbs, and place them on a plate.

5. Place the ravioli in the air fryer basket in an even layer, then mist them lightly with olive oil.

6. Air fry at 400°F (204°C) 4 minutes. Flip the ravioli over, mist them lightly with olive oil, then cook them for another 3 minutes until crispy.

7. Serve ravioli with warm marinara sauce.

Notes

- This recipe is designed for a 16 L rack-style air fryer or 25 L rack-style air fryer.

- If you are using a 4 L basket-style air fryer or 12 L basket-style air fryer, cook the ravioli in 3-4 batches.

Tips

1. Leave 1/4-inch (6.5 mm) of space between each ravioli to prevent them from becoming soggy.

2. Do not use frozen ravioli. Let them thaw first to ensure they are fully cooked after 7 minutes.

NUTRITION INFO

SERVING SIZE: 8 RAVIOLIS

Calories	360 kcal
Carbohydrates	45.7 g
Fats	12 g
Protein	16 g
Sugar	9.5 g
Sodium	676 mg
Cholesterol	94 mg

SIMPLE CHEDDAR HERB BREAD

Prep Time
10 MINUTES

Cook Time
15 MINUTES

Total Time
25 MINUTES

Serves
12

INGREDIENTS

- Olive oil, for misting
- 2 cups (240 grams) whole wheat flour
- 4 teaspoons (19 grams) baking powder
- 1 tablespoon (12 grams) granulated sugar
- 1 1/2 teaspoons (8 grams) garlic powder
- 1/2 teaspoon (3 grams) onion powder
- 2 tablespoons fresh (8 grams) parsley, minced
- 2 tablespoons (5 grams) fresh chives, minced
- 1/2 teaspoon (3 grams) kosher salt
- 3/4 cup (62 grams) shredded cheddar cheese
- 3 tablespoons (45 ml) unsalted butter, melted
- 1 large egg
- 1 cup (224 grams) buttermilk

INSTRUCTIONS

1. Preheat the air fryer to 320°F (160°C).
2. Mist 2 mini silicone loaf pans with olive oil and set them aside.
3. Whisk whole wheat flour, baking powder, granulated sugar, garlic powder, onion powder, parsley, chives, and kosher salt in a large bowl until combined.
4. Add the cheddar cheese to the dry ingredients and mix until combined.
5. Whisk the melted butter, egg, and buttermilk in a separate bowl until combined, then pour it into the dry ingredients. Mix until combined.
6. Divide the batter between 2 mini silicone loaf pans and air fry at 320°F (160°C) for 12-15 minutes until a skewer inserted into the center of the cheddar herb bread comes out clean.

Notes

- This recipe is designed for a 12 L basket-style air fryer, 16 L rack-style air fryer, or 25 L rack-style air fryer.
- If you are using a 4 L basket-style air fryer, cook the bread 1 loaf at a time.

Tips

1. Do not overmix the cheddar herb bread batter, or else the bread will be tough.
2. Let the cheddar herb bread cool completely in the pan before slicing, or it will crumble when you try to cut it.

NUTRITION INFO

SERVING SIZE: 1 SLICE OF CHEDDAR HERB BREAD

Calories	70 kcal
Carbohydrates	6 g
Fats	4.1 g
Protein	2.5 g
Sugar	1.4 g
Sodium	71 mg
Cholesterol	26 mg

BLUEBERRY LEMON BREAD

Prep Time	Cook Time	Total Time	Serves
5 MINUTES	20 MINUTES	25 MINUTES	8

INGREDIENTS

- Avocado oil, for misting
- 1 1/2 cups (180 grams) whole wheat flour
- 1 teaspoon (5 grams) baking powder
- 1/4 teaspoon (1.5 grams) fine sea salt
- Zest of 1 lemon
- 1/2 cup (108 ml) coconut oil, melted
- 3/4 cup (150 grams) granulated sugar
- 2 large eggs
- 1/2 cup (120 ml) buttermilk
- Juice of 1/2 lemon
- 1 1/2 cups (285 grams) fresh blueberries

INSTRUCTIONS

1. Preheat the air fryer to 320°F (160°C).
2. Grease an air fryer loaf pan lightly with avocado oil.
3. Whisk whole wheat flour, baking powder, sea salt, and lemon zest in a large bowl until combined.
4. Whisk the coconut oil, granulated sugar, eggs, buttermilk, and lemon juice in another bowl until combined.
5. Add the wet ingredients to the flour mixture and mix until combined.
6. Fold in the fresh blueberries, then pour it into the prepared loaf pan.
7. Air fry at 320°F (160°C) for 20 minutes until a toothpick inserted into the bread comes out clean.

Notes

- This recipe is designed for a 12 L basket-style air fryer, 16 L rack-style air fryer, or 25 L rack-style air fryer.
- If you are using a 4 L basket-style air fryer, cook the blueberry lemon bread in 2 silicone mini loaf pans one at a time.

Tips

1. Do not overmix the blueberry lemon bread batter, or else the bread will be tough.
2. If the blueberry lemon bread is still not cooked after 20 minutes, air fry it for another 5 minutes until a skewer inserted into the cake comes out clean.

NUTRITION INFO

SERVING SIZE: 1 SLICE OF BLUEBERRY LEMON BREAD

Calories	147 kcal
Carbohydrates	17.6 g
Fats	7.7 g
Protein	3.3 g
Sugar	11.1 g
Sodium	56 mg
Cholesterol	45 mg

CLASSIC PIZZA BAGELS

Prep Time
5 MINUTES

Cook Time
4 MINUTES

Total Time
9 MINUTES

Serves
4

INGREDIENTS

- 4 whole wheat bagels
- ½ cup (120 grams) pizza sauce
- ½ cup (69 grams) pepperoni
- ½ cup (112 grams) shredded mozzarella cheese
- 1/2 teaspoon dried (1 gram) oregano
- 1/2 teaspoon (0.5 grams) crushed red pepper flakes, optional

INSTRUCTIONS

1. Preheat the air fryer to 370°F (187°C).
2. Place the bagels on a plate and spread 2 tablespoons of pizza sauce on each bagel, then divide the pepperoni slices between each bagel.
3. Add 2 tablespoons (30 grams) of mozzarella cheese to each bagel. Line the air fryer basket or tray with parchment paper, then add the pizza bagels.
4. Air fry at 370°F (187°C) for 4 minutes until the cheese melts, then garnish with oregano and crushed red pepper flakes.

NUTRITION INFO

SERVING SIZE: 1 PIZZA BAGEL

Calories	147 kcal
Carbohydrates	17.6 g
Fats	7.7 g
Protein	3.3 g
Sugar	11.1 g
Sodium	56 mg
Cholesterol	45 mg

Notes

- This recipe is designed for a 12 L basket-style air fryer, 16 L rack-style air fryer, or 25 L rack-style air fryer.
- If you are using a 4 L basket-style air fryer, cook the pizza bagels one at a time.

Tips

1. Do not place the pepperoni slices on top of the mozzarella cheese. Placing the mozzarella cheese on top of the pepperoni keeps it weighed down and prevents it from flying around in the air fryer.
2. Do not add too much pizza sauce to the pizza bagels, or they will be soggy.

CLASSIC MOZZARELLA STICKS

Prep Time
10 MINUTES

Cook Time
7 MINUTES

Total Time
17 MINUTES

Serves
4

INGREDIENTS

- 1/4 cup (30 grams) whole wheat flour
- 2 large eggs
- 1 tablespoon (15 ml) water
- ½ cup (60 grams) whole wheat bread crumbs
- ½ cup (60 grams) Panko bread crumbs
- 1 teaspoon (1 gram) dried parsley
- 1 teaspoon (5 grams) kosher salt
- 1/2 teaspoon (3 grams) black pepper
- 1 teaspoon (5 grams) garlic powder
- 1/2 teaspoon (3 grams) onion powder
- 8 pieces of mozzarella string cheese, cut in half vertically
- 1/2 cup (112 grams) warm marinara sauce for serving

INSTRUCTIONS

1. Preheat the air fryer to 390°F (198°C).
2. Place the whole wheat flour in a shallow baking dish.
3. Mix the eggs and water in a small bowl until combined.
4. Mix the whole wheat bread crumbs, Panko bread crumbs, parsley, kosher salt, black pepper, and garlic and onion powder in another shallow baking dish.
5. Dredge each piece of cheese in the flour, then in the egg, then in the breadcrumbs.
6. Place the mozzarella sticks in the air fryer basket or tray in an even layer and air fry at 390°F (198°C) for 5-7 minutes until golden brown.

Notes

- This recipe is designed for a 12 L basket-style air fryer, 16 L rack-style air fryer, or 25 L rack-style air fryer.
- If you are using a 4 L basket-style air fryer, cook the mozzarella sticks in 2 batches.

Tips

1. Press the breadcrumbs into the cheese to form a thick coating. This will prevent the cheese from escaping.
2. Check the mozzarella sticks halfway through cooking; if the cheese is melted, they are cooked.

NUTRITION INFO

SERVING SIZE: 4 MOZZARELLA STICKS

Calories	210 kcal
Carbohydrates	9.4 g
Fats	11.1 g
Protein	20.1 g
Sugar	0.9 g
Sodium	534 mg
Cholesterol	104 mg